Rethinking Public Administration

RETHINKING POLITICAL SCIENCE AND INTERNATIONAL STUDIES

This series is a forum for innovative scholarly writing from across all substantive fields of political science and international studies. The series aims to enrich the study of these fields by promoting a cutting-edge approach to thought and analysis. Academic scrutiny and challenge is an essential component in the development of political science and international studies as fields of study, and the act of re-thinking and re-examining principles and precepts that may have been long-held is imperative.

Rethinking Political Science and International Studies showcases authored books that address the field from a new angle, expose the weaknesses of existing concepts and arguments, or 're-frame' the topic in some way. This might be through the introduction of radical ideas, through the integration of perspectives from other fields or even disciplines, through challenging existing paradigms, or simply through a level of analysis that elevates or sharpens our understanding of a subject.

For a full list of Edward Elgar published titles, including the titles in this series, visit our website at www.e-elgar.com.

Rethinking Public Administration

Marc Holzer

*Professor Emeritus and Founding Dean, School of Public
Affairs and Administration, Rutgers University; Distinguished
Research Professor, Institute for Public Service, Suffolk
University-Boston; Elected Fellow, National Academy of Public
Administration, USA*

RETHINKING POLITICAL SCIENCE AND
INTERNATIONAL STUDIES

Edward **Elgar**
PUBLISHING

Cheltenham, UK • Northampton, MA, USA

Published by
Edward Elgar Publishing Limited
The Lypiatts
15 Lansdown Road
Cheltenham
Glos GL50 2JA
UK

Edward Elgar Publishing, Inc.
William Pratt House
9 Dewey Court
Northampton
Massachusetts 01060
USA

A catalogue record for this book
is available from the British Library

Library of Congress Control Number: 2023939952

This book is available electronically in the **Elgar**online
Political Science and Public Policy subject collection
http://dx.doi.org/10.4337/9781789907094

ISBN 978 1 78990 708 7 (cased)
ISBN 978 1 78990 709 4 (eBook)

Printed and bound in Great Britain by
TJ Books Limited, Padstow, Cornwall

This volume is dedicated to the memory of Professor Frederick S. Lane, an exceptional scholar who significantly strengthened our understanding of public organizations and a gifted teacher who inspired many students to pursue careers in public service.

Contents

Boxes

Acknowledgements

Most projects are team efforts, and that is certainly true of this project. *Rethinking Public Administration* only became a reality with the support of many exceptional individuals.

First and foremost is my wife Mady, who was consistently supportive, patient and encouraging, as she has been for over five decades.

Many of my fellow academic colleagues helped me conceptualize my arguments herein, in particular Frederick S. Lane, who recently passed away and to whom this book is dedicated.

My research for this book is very much a function of collaboration with faculty nationally and internationally, especially: Elaine Yi Lu, Brenda Bond Fortier, Stephanie Newbold, Norma Riccucci and Prajapati Trivedi. That research has been supported by former doctoral students with whom I first worked on the themes inherent in this book. They have since become esteemed colleagues: Andrew Ballard, Daniel Bromberg, Vatche Gabrielian, Iryna Illiash, Patria deLancer Julnes, Aroon Manoharan, Lois Warner and Kaifeng Yang. I am equally indebted to the graduate fellows who supported my research at Suffolk University's Institute for Public Service, in particular: Ian Gawthrop, Mallory Sullivan and Joshua Weissman-LaFrance.

The integrity of this manuscript in terms of citations and facts, and its clarity in terms of language, are an author's responsibility and an editor's trade; I was fortunate to have had the excellent assistance of a smart, skilled editorial assistant in validating this manuscript: Jonathan Wexler.

The inception of this project came at the invitation of Harry Fabian, the Acquisitions Editor at Edward Elgar, to pursue a volume by this title. He has been especially understanding as the Covid pandemic almost immediately intervened and certainly eroded my momentum. His patience is as admirable as much as his comments are invaluable. My thanks to everyone at Edward Elgar who have worked to bring this book to the point of publication.

Marc Holzer

1. Introduction to *Rethinking Public Administration*: in pursuit of the public good

The audacity that I could "rethink" an established field, a field laden with many insightful academics and practitioners, is a humbling task. Public administration as a field of study and practice is at least a century-and-a-half old, although it is more likely the result of a process of continuous thought and improvement dating back several millennia.

Throughout the world and throughout history, empires and kingdoms have required large public organizations, or bureaucracies. Bureaucrats were the necessary problem solvers for building and administering military and canal systems, roads and bridges, taxation and justice arrangements, census and statistical records, and all other governmental functions.

When I came to the study of public administration almost six decades ago, the modern field of public administration was well established in university schools, scholarly books and peer-reviewed journals. Public management was positioned as the product of reasoned, characteristically scientific, insights. Behavior was circumscribed by rules and standards. Government was respected more so than it is today.

As I helped to build the body of knowledge that practitioners would need to implement public policies, to deliver on government's promises, public skepticism of government became increasingly apparent. Only a few academics came forward to counter that skepticism. Chief among them was Charles T. Goodsell who made *The Case for Bureaucracy*. Describing his book as a polemic or "controversial argument," Goodsell related that "I have come to believe – with some intensity – that the quality of governmental administration in America has been greatly misrepresented in this country's popular commentary and academic discourse. My purpose is to counter this wrong" (Goodsell, 1994 [2014]). His argument resonated with me and with the field. It is very much an inspiration for my own work and especially for this book.

Goodsell's work has inspired many others. For example, Douglas J. Amy provides excellent evidence in *Government Is Good* (Amy, 2011), now a website under the same title (governmentisgood.com), that:

> The public sector is also how we provide for essential human needs that are neglected by the market – such as clean air and water, safe workplaces, and economic security. What's more, government serves as an important instrument of moral action – a way for us to rectify injustices, eliminate suffering, and care for each other. If we want an America that is prosperous, healthy, secure, well-educated, just, compassionate, and unpolluted, we need a strong, active, and well-funded public sector.

Yet, according to the Pew Research Center, trust in government has declined precipitously in the US, from about 60–70 percent in the early 1960s to 20–25 percent early in 2021; the decline cuts across all cohorts: Gen Z, Millennial, Gen X, Boomer, Silent, Greatest (https://trustgov.net/dataexpplorers).

That deterioration in the public's trust is somewhat of a conundrum as research has produced convincing evidence that public servants produce services efficiently and with many successes in achieving intended impacts. The US federal government publishes such data daily. Many jurisdictions collect and post performance data. Hundreds, if not thousands, of state and local programs are recognized annually for their achievements. Thousands of public servants are honored by their agencies and their professional associations for exceptional efforts in program leadership and innovation. A large body of evidence is illustrative of effective government, but it rarely captures the public's attention, or that of their media surrogates. Too many candidates for office routinely dwell on atypical incidents of waste and abuse without acknowledging the day-to-day, routine accomplishments of the public workforce.

The successes achieved by public servants are simply not apparent to citizens who absorb the media's pervasive, primarily negative, images. The image of civil servants suffers from guilt by association, from confusion with the misdeeds of their political superiors. Although the public service in the US is among the most honest in the world, the reputation of appointed civil servants is diminished due to inept or inefficient actions of elected "public servants." The press features charges of misconduct under headlines such as "Local Official Indicted" or "Public Servant Accused." Typically, the official in question is likely to have been an elected official or a political appointee, not a civil servant. Such simple headlines taint the entire public service by association with their sometimes-unethical political taskmasters. The average reader is not likely to differentiate between political office holders and their merit-based careerists. Because corruption anywhere in government tarnishes the image of anyone in government, the reputation of civil servants is diminished by mis-identification with less-than-ethical politicians. As the press dutifully chronicles charges of misconduct against elected officials and politicians, it often unintentionally taints career civil servants and their agencies with pejorative terms such as bureaucratic, unethical, uncaring, incompetent and faceless. As a result, cynicism increases and trust declines. The field needs to present evidence to the public that society is well served by those who staff government.

We must also broaden our tent, so to speak. The field of public administration should adopt a broad definition of public service as a continuum of contributions. The public is well served by those who staff not only government, but government's partners in service to the public: nonprofits, volunteers, the media, foundations, donor-advised funds, public-private partnerships and related entities. Those de facto public servants represent a very large segment of the workforce, perhaps as much as 40 percent, and more if we count part-time volunteers working on behalf of their neighbors. Their efforts provide critical support for our economy and our personal lives. In the US there are more than 90,000 units of government, federal, state, local and special purpose employing well over 20 million people. There are almost two million nonprofit organizations. Millions of citizens serve the public as employees in, and contractors for, government, nonprofit and related entities. Over 75 million adults, plus many millions of high school and college students, volunteer annually. They are all providing public service and should all be identified and praised as such. *Public servant* is a positive term; *bureaucrat* is not.

Public service is often described as a noble, ethical calling, and the public needs to be reminded of it as such. At his inauguration, John Fitzgerald Kennedy, the 35th President of the United States, famously issued a call to serve: "And so, my fellow Americans, ask not what your country can do for you: ask what you can do for your country." During his administration he cast public service as "a proud and lively career." George H.W. Bush, the 41st President, held that "Public service is a noble calling, and we need men and women of character to believe that they can make a difference in their communities, in their states and in their country." Representative Lee H. Hamilton, a former member of Congress and Chairman of the 9/11 Commission, said it as well as anyone:

> I can assure you, public service is a stimulating, proud and lively enterprise. It is not just a way of life. It is a way to live fully. Its greatest attraction is the sheer challenge of it – struggling to find solutions to the great issues of the day. It can fulfill your highest aspirations. The call to service is one of the highest callings you will hear and your country can make.

Marty Walsh, Mayor of Boston and subsequently Secretary of Labor in the Biden Administration, cast service to the public as a career-defining passion:

> Public service comes in many forms. It starts wherever you are and whatever you're doing, no matter how humble your first job or your second job or your third job is.

> If you give yourself to serve others, you will have an impact. You will move in the
> direction of your dreams. (Holzer, 2021)

Contrary to the automatic and negative attribution of "bureaucrat," public
servants have been "good bureaucrats," quietly absorbing criticisms and
professionally persevering. They work under difficult, even dangerous, circumstances. Fatalities and injuries occur to a greater extent than is commonly
assumed by the image of desk-bound paper pushers. Public servants often
place themselves in the path of danger, sometime losing their lives. This is
most apparent in the military or emergency services, but also when protecting
students in the classroom, maintaining roads and transit, fighting forest fires,
serving in diplomatic missions or the peace corps, treating patients with com-
municable diseases and confronting many other hazards. Each year hundreds
of law enforcement and emergency workers are fatally injured; hundreds of
thousands suffer nonfatal injuries and illnesses. Road maintenance workers
have an even higher incidence of risk of death and injury. Teachers are increasingly under attack physically. Among social workers, health providers and
public health personnel, their physical and mental health is compromised by
aggressive clients, unsafe environments or toxic substances they are detecting.

A long series of dialogues with my students and other practitioners
convinced me that they were making inordinate sacrifices for the public good,
committing themselves to elevating the lives of their fellow citizens at lower
salaries and in more difficult circumstances than their private sector counterparts. The academic public administration community convinced me that
important insights were being developed almost daily. In contrast, however,
even colleagues in the closely related academic fields of political science and
business/management succumbed to unfounded assumptions about the public
sector workforce and its capacities or achievements. Following the media
convinced me that good government was not newsworthy. Listening to political rhetoric convinced me that their complaints about bureaucracy were almost
always without foundation, although they did resonate with many readers and
voters. Dialogue with relatives convinced me that baseless stereotypes were
held by even well-educated citizens.

Those experiences helped define four avenues of research, each of which
is represented in this book as a set of opportunities to rethink how the field of
public administration might reposition itself as society's necessary and best
investments. Admittedly, the ability to counter unfair portraits is constrained
by laws that prohibit proactive "public relations" efforts by government
agencies, permitting only passive and relatively plain dissemination of "public
information." Within those constraints, the public administration community
of academics and practitioners needs to rebuild trust to the levels of five
decades ago by pursuing new strategies. How might we reverse this downward

drift by addressing our critics and reassuring our citizens? Do those critics have something to offer, or are they simply uninformed or given over to stereotyping society's public servants? Are we missing the import of their messages, thereby constraining our performance? Are we failing to present the evidence of high performing government? Can we do a better job of avoiding problems?

Chapter 2, "Admirable Intent, Critical Reviews," is a set of propositions that the arts and humanities have long been raising about bureaucracy's unintended impacts on those who have chosen to serve the public. They caution that bureaucrats are themselves the victims of their own bureaucratic environs, transforming characteristically energetic, innovative public servants who are eager to serve into jaded organizational components. Recurring themes in fiction and on the screen are that life within the organization – public or private – is one in which people have internalized counterproductive values: an overemphasis on formality, on rules and regulations, on security, on a culture epitomized by the sufficiency of mediocrity and the adage "don't rock the boat." New recruits are characterized as quickly learning that there are few positive rewards, and many risks or sanctions, for individuals who challenge entrenched assumptions and old beliefs, take risks and hold ethics above organizational interests. At the least, they become stifled, losing all sense of independence, pride and initiative. The dangers of becoming a bureaucrat are particularly evident in those who are demoralized, who no longer care, who go through the motions, who count down the years until retirement. As employees, they are the "deadwood" which clients so often decry. They are bureaucracy's victims as well as its instruments. Unable to utilize their problem-solving energies productively within the bureaucracy, they turn elsewhere – to family, hobbies, community organizations. Of equal concern, their energies as workers and managers may be corrupted, rather than merely suppressed. Without the possibility of solving problems productively, they may direct energies to personal profit, to gaining promotion, to playing office politics, to abusing and discrediting clients and fellow employees. They too often find themselves discouraged.

Of course, the arts and humanities have also captured the public's frustrations with the seemingly inexplicable and unjust actions of bureaucrats. Most frustrated clients – individuals or representatives of aggrieved groups – have never been made aware of effective, albeit unorthodox, tactics for pursuing those battles. Authors and artists, however, have agency to do so, and often sketch out those strategies just short of the law. Their work explores dozens of strategies for securing remediation from organizations, typically strategies too outlandish to be replicated, but which can serve to alert us to the unintended consequences of rigid, confined thinking. Organizations work best with practiced discretion, but work worst within unthinking routines.

Critical commentaries on the harm generated by our large organizations – public and private – are found from short stories to novels, streaming cable series to movies, cartoons to serious art. As a field, however, we have taken little note of those critiques. It would be to our advantage to do so, especially in the public administration classroom, webinars, blogs and social media. We should endeavor to recognize positive examples of dedication and sacrifice, examples that are abundantly evident in the unorthodox media such as criminal justice and public hospital dramas. The field can leverage those examples, most powerfully evident on large and small screens, to build more appreciation for public service careers and for those who make great sacrifices for the public good.

Chapter 3, "Delivering Performance, as Promised," argues that the public sector is innovative and competent. It performs at high levels, and efficiently so.

Performance measurement and management serve several purposes. To successfully operate their organizations, public managers need specific, diagnostic information. This applies to all management levels within all public service organizations. Performance measurement must be considered a requisite and critical part of the management process. Managers could use the data that performance measures provide to help them manage in three basic ways: to account for past activities, to manage current operations, or to assess progress toward planned objectives. When used to look at past activities, performance measures can show the accountability of processes and procedures used to complete a task, as well as program results. When used to manage current operations, performance measures can show how efficiently resources, such as dollars and staff, are being used. Finally, when tied to planned objectives, performance measures can be used to assess how effectively an agency is achieving the goals stated in its long-range strategic plan. Having well-designed measures that are timely, relevant and accurate is important, but it is also important that the measures actually be used by decision-makers to improve services.

Performance management – beginning with measures that highlight accomplishments, problems and opportunities – can contribute to the following advantages:

- Improved decision-making: Performance measures afford managers needed information to execute their control functions, improving efficiencies, cutting costs, and investing in more effective service delivery systems.
- Performance assessment: The measures connect individual and organizational performance to the management of employees, serving as a means of motivation.
- Accountability: The performance process engenders managerial responsibility, especially in budget construction and implementation.

- Service delivery: The performance improvement process improves timeliness and effectiveness, helping position programs as worthy of future investments and as examples of future cost avoidance.
- Public participation: Performance reporting can influence the citizenry to care more about public workers' efforts to improve service delivery, thereby helping to build stakeholder support for increases in future budget cycles.
- Improvement of civic discourse: Making public discussions about public service delivery factual and data based, more responsible fiscal decisions are likely to result.

Improvement strategies that have been developed by the most effective leaders of the most productive public organizations are fairly sophisticated, and several such "roadmaps" for measuring and improving performance are drawn from the literature and from practice. Rather than reinventing performance plans on an idiosyncratic basis, performance leaders should identify the most appropriate elements from each and proceed with blended plans of their own. We expect that the evident sophistication and outcomes of those plans, and repeated citations of award-winning best practices and exemplary programs, will surprise our critics and begin to help rebuild the public's trust. Performance data will very likely demonstrate that public sector productivity and improvement rates are often equal to or better than those in the private sector.

Chapter 4, "Bureaucratic Resistance as Ethical Persistence," is written from the assumption that public organizations, as bureaucracies, are characteristically and willfully blind to internal criticisms. Those public servants who we might term "bureaucratic resisters" often raise important questions about factual premises for mandated actions, dangers to the public and to employees, ethical transgressions and other threats to the organization and its missions. We define nearly 20 strategies that resisters have followed; not all resulted in immediate successes, but on a long-term basis all added momentum to the practice of ethical, effective government. Our premise is that this body of cases indicates that it is all to the advantage of public bureaucracies to listen without prejudice, possibly avoiding expensive and reputation-damaging situations. Many successful cases provide assurances to public servants that "blowing the whistle" does not mean blowing their jobs.

In terms of practicality and morality, bureaucratic "guerillas" are cautioned as to futile, dead-end tactics. Because we should not replace the evils of organizational arrogance with the those of instrumentality, the public administration field must clearly advise against tactics that assume the ends justify any convenient means. The subfield of administrative ethics deserves more prominence as a rich vein of such advice.

Chapter 5, "Businesslike Government, but Not as a Business," confronts the popular notion that government should be run according to the principles of the private sector. The business model follows from the persistent myth that government is inefficient and unbusinesslike. That rationale for privatization has gained momentum, degrading the public sector's capacity to continue to innovate. Countering that rush to privatization, a model that is dubious and ineffective, public administration academics have long held that government and business are distinctly different. Those cautions have not, however, impeded privatization's momentum. We propose an alternative model of competition within the public sector – government vs. government – open only to public agencies. That experiment would establish "generic" agencies that have performance (efficient and effective services) as their mission – analogous to "profit" in the private sector. It would mirror business conglomerates, but only under the umbrella of public sector values. It would implement the advantages of competition by establishing Agencies A, B, C, etc. as eligible bidders on any public service, ignoring the silos and rigidities of the traditional governmental organization chart. The public sector certainly has the experience and capacities to build and utilize this alternative. And regardless of what management model is applied to the delivery of public services, those managing in the public sphere require a basic knowledge of the full range of competencies necessary to do so: personal fundamentals, leading change, leading people, focusing on results, applying management processes, integrating necessary resources, and building coalitions. Too few hold Master of Public Administration (MPA degrees), and even those who do are unlikely to have a full toolkit of public management skills. Public management competency frameworks vary, but all are based on the assumption that the job is complex and differs from the private sector in many important respects. Too many programs and agencies are run by professionals such as doctors, lawyers, engineers, teachers with service-specific licenses or certifications, but virtually no trained competencies as public managers.

Chapter 6, "A Comeback for the Administrative State," concludes with an argument that the field of public administration must actively refute the negative connotations of labels such as "deep state." We should argue that keeping constitutional, legislative and political promises to our citizens requires an efficient, effective and ethical executive branch. The private sector alternative is not acceptable as its guiding principles are distinctly different from those in the public sphere. Within the umbrella of government's value propositions we need to be proactive in addressing core concerns in order to reestablish the need for competent, effective and ethical administration of policy implementation.

TAKEAWAYS

Declining trust in government can be reversed, and to do so the field of public administration must:

- Confront toxic stereotypes.
- Greatly broaden the identity of the term public servant.
- Present evidence that government delivers, as promised.
- Attribute legitimacy to bureaucracy's internal critics.
- Confront the myths of the business model.

SELECTIONS FOR FURTHER READING AND RESEARCH

Amy, Douglas J. Government is good. https://governmentisgood.com
Makes a compelling argument in defense of the public sector's efficacy in continuously improving the public good.

Goodsell, C. (1994) *The New Case for Bureaucracy*. Washington, DC: CQ Press.
Argues that the US public sector is effective and innovative, delivering on promised services and thereby maintaining the legitimacy of a democracy in the minds of its citizenry.

Holzer, M. (1999) *Public Service: Callings, Commitments, and Contributions*. New York and London: Routledge.
Captures a long, continuing debate as to the health of the public service, and in so doing suggests agendas for university research and administrative action.

Holzer, M. and Schwester, R.W. (2020) *Public Administration: An Introduction*. Third edition. New York and London: Routledge.
Enlivens the teaching of public administration, improves the learning experience, and helps motivate students of public service to become problem-solving public servants.

REFERENCES

Amy, D. J. (2011) *Government Is Good*. Indianapolis: Dog Ear Publishing.
Goodsell, C.T. (1994) *The Case for Bureaucracy*. Third edition. Chatham, NJ: Chatham Press.
Goodsell, C.T. (2014) *The New Case for Bureaucracy*. Washington, DC: CQ Press.
Holzer, M. (2021) *A Call to Serve: Quotes on Public Service*. Washington, DC: American Society for Public Administration. https://trustgov.net/dataexpplorers

2.　Admirable intent, critical reviews

THE PUBLIC GOOD AS THE FOUNDATION OF PUBLIC ADMINISTRATION

The foundational ethos of government is dedication to the public good. For millennia, people have mutually consented to form governments – from tribes to kingdoms to nations – to provide for necessary common services. Public organizations came to include the military for national security; police and fire for the protection of lives and property; roads, canals and bridges to facilitate commerce and agriculture; hospitals and public health measures to support wellbeing and suppress epidemics; and taxes or fees as a prerequisite to support for the many services that enhance everyone's quality of life.

Public administration organizations provide for the collective wellbeing by implementing their government's promises for:

- Security and Defense
- Social Order
- Commerce: Currency, Dispute Resolution, Mail, Roads, Ports
- Regulation: Safety, Quality, Fairness
- Education: Primary, Secondary and Post-secondary
- Health and Social Services
- Public Health
- International Relations
- Libraries, Recreation/Parks
- And many other functions.

To deliver those necessary public services, citizens have sworn to answer the call to serve their fellows and families. The citizens of ancient Athens (restricted to men) vowed to act ethically, pledging to The Athenian Oath, and today's public servants would be well reminded of that commitment, cast in stone at the entrance to Syracuse University's Maxwell School of Citizenship and Public Affairs:

> We will never bring disgrace to this our city by any act of dishonesty or cowardice
> … we will revere and obey the city's laws and do our best to incite a like respect
> in those above us who are prone to annul or set them at naught; we will strive

unceasingly to quicken the public's sense of civic duty. Thus, in all these ways, we will transmit this city not only, not less, but greater and more beautiful than it was transmitted to us. (Holzer, 2018)

Today, oaths of office are commonly sworn to. In the US elected and appointed officials swear to uphold the US Constitution, and often a state constitution as well, as well as a code specific to their profession. A model is the American Society for Public Administration's (ASPA) Code of Ethics potentially applicable to all appointed public servants, incorporating the intent and standards of oaths of office across the public sector (American Society for Public Administration, 2022):

> The American Society for Public Administration (ASPA) advances the science, art, and practice of public administration. The Society affirms its responsibility to develop the spirit of responsible professionalism within its membership and to increase awareness and commitment to ethical principles and standards among all those who work in public service in all sectors. To this end, the members of the Society, commit ourselves to uphold the following principles:
>
> Advance the Public Interest. Promote the interests of the public and put service to the public above service to oneself.
>
> Uphold the Constitution and the Law. Respect and support government constitutions and laws, while seeking to improve laws and policies to promote the public good.
>
> Promote democratic participation. Inform the public and encourage active engagement in governance. Be open, transparent and responsive, and respect and assist all persons in their dealings with public organizations.
>
> Strengthen social equity. Treat all persons with fairness, justice, and equality and respect individual differences, rights, and freedoms. Promote affirmative action and other initiatives to reduce unfairness, injustice, and inequality in society.
>
> Fully Inform and Advise. Provide accurate, honest, comprehensive, and timely information and advice to elected and appointed officials and governing board members, and to staff members in your organization.
>
> Demonstrate personal integrity. Adhere to the highest standards of conduct to inspire public confidence and trust in public service.
>
> Promote Ethical Organizations: Strive to attain the highest standards of ethics, stewardship, and public service in organizations that serve the public.
>
> Advance Professional Excellence: Strengthen personal capabilities to act competently and ethically and encourage the professional development of others.

Such oaths of office, grounded in the ethos of the public good and the ethics of honest, fair administration are evident in many professions of public service. Police officers, for example, typically swear to an oath such as that authored by the International Association of Chiefs of Police (IACP):

> On my honor, I will never betray my profession, my integrity, my character or the public trust. I will always have the courage to hold myself and others accountable

for our actions. I will always uphold the laws of my country, my community and the agency I serve. (Oath of Office, 2020)

Teachers are committed to a Code of Ethics (1975/2020) published by the National Education Association:

- Commitment to the Student: The educator strives to help each student realize his or her potential as a worthy and effective member of society. The educator therefore works to stimulate the spirit of inquiry, the acquisition of knowledge and understanding, and the thoughtful formulation of worthy goals.
- Commitment to the Profession: The education profession is vested by the public with a trust and responsibility requiring the highest ideals of professional service. In the belief that the quality of the services of the education professional directly influences the nation and its citizens, the educator shall exert every effort to raise professional standards, to promote a climate that encourages the exercise of professional judgment, to achieve the conditions that attract person worthy of the trust to careers in education, and to assist in preventing the practice of the professional by unqualified persons (NEA, 2020).

Today, although the subject of ethics has indeed become a part of public administration curricula and practice, it is insufficiently emphasized, leaving future public servants ill equipped to confront the dilemmas they will undoubtedly encounter. There are textbooks and a *Journal of Public Integrity*. Ethics training is often mandated for public servants but learning about ethics typically ends with the degree or an in-service, online training video that incorporates brief scenarios. Those resources are necessary and important. They are, however, insufficient for career-long, indeed lifelong, awareness of the ethical dilemmas that inevitably confront public servants in their professional roles, conundrums that extend to uncompensated roles as public servants serving as elected officials, as volunteers or as board members.

Oaths of office and Ethics Codes are powerful guidelines in principle, but not always practiced. Those who serve the public are best served by continuous learning that assists them in avoiding ethical transgressions. The public is best served by public servants who have thought through the dilemmas and conundrums they might face, and immediately know what actions are correct, honest and fair, and what are incorrect, dishonest or biased.

ETHICAL MESSAGES FROM THE ARTS AND HUMANITIES

A largely overlooked resource for addressing that ethical "awareness gap" is thoughtful exposure to the ethical commentaries offered by the arts and humanities, especially in terms of awareness of toxic behaviors, practices and cultures that damage or constrain clients and colleagues. Such commentaries serve as early and continuing alerts to problems that traditional scholarship is missing or minimizing. They can engage present and future public servants in increasing their awareness of ethical dilemmas. They can deepen an awareness of the conundrums that public servants confront in adhering to ethical guidelines. A cultivated sensitivity to those commentaries can help public servants act properly, and always in the public interest.

Random, unstructured contact with a wide range of "Unorthodox" administrative commentary – the Bible, novels, short fiction, poetry, Greek and Shakespearean theatre, drama and musicals, music, statuary, cinema and television and streaming series – can all inform the practice of public administration, but they are rarely introduced into the curriculum. An individual's engaging and lifelong encounters with those critiques, however, might well trigger their own capacities for insight and reflection.

Management issues with ethical implications, especially with regard to leadership, accountability and personnel management, have been treated in literature since ancient times. Set in the public or private sector, they offer important lessons for practitioners. Sophocles' Antigone and Homer's "Iliad" deal with issues of leadership and administrative style, discipline and morale in an organization. Shakespeare's insights into management theory date to the early seventeenth century, offering an invaluable source for managerial lessons, and are condensed in Box 2.1.

BOX 2.1   BUREAUCRACY AND THE BARD

Excerpted from *Public Voices* Vol. 14, No. 2, 2015

Symposium editor: Aaron Wachhaus
Shakespeare's work continues to appeal due to his masterful exploration of the human element at work in complex settings. Of particular relevance to public administration, and emphasized in these articles, are the following themes:

First, the acknowledgement that the human element deeply impacts the operation of the machinery of government. Lear was an apparently successful king. He had been a competent administrator of the machinery of his state. However, his need to be loved, not for his technical accomplishments but for his own sake, led to the downfall of his reign, the destruction of his family, and chaos in the land. Similarly, Henry V is compelling not because of his accomplishments on the battlefield or as a ruler, but because of his refusal to quietly give up his individualism and assume totally the functionalism of a working monarch. For Henry, to become the state is to lose part of his humanity. As Shakespeare shows us, it is precisely his individuality that informs his rule.

Second, the recognition that multiple perspectives are necessary to obtain a full view. Shakespeare presents vivid characters with strong drives and goals operating in complex social webs. They face complicated problems. We, the audience, benefit from seeing the action at a remove that allows us to take in the unintended consequences of individual action, as well as from hearing and seeing multiple perspectives from a variety of characters. Our distance from the stage allows us to see Kate Minola as both empowered woman as well as titular Shrew. Frequently, Shakespearean plays turn on the inability of characters to step outside their own, often self-imposed, constraints and speak openly and broadly. Hamlet would be a much shorter and less bloody affair were the prince of Denmark able to talk openly about the problems in his family and country. Over and over again, Shakespeare shows us the consequences of initially simple or small deceptions, inversions or omissions. Surely, there must have been some moment when Othello and Desdemona could simply have confronted one another honestly and openly. Shakespearean comedies rely on our ability to see past deceptions that, while quite transparent to us, envelop the characters. Too often in public administration, we lack the ability to gain sufficient distance to step outside ourselves, take in our situation from a range of viewpoints and increase transparency.

Finally, the development of narrative across several levels at once. For Shakespeare, sub-text drives the play as much as does the overt level of dialogue and action. As Farmer notes, "Important lessons from Shakespeare come not so much from the surface but from the subterranean, not so much from the main story as the incidental". We, as readers and audience members, benefit from being able to take in the larger play, making connections that are not apparent from the stage and gaining a broader and deeper understanding of the play as a whole. As administrators, we cannot effectively understand complex problems while immersed in them. A single perspective is, by its nature, limiting. Responsible management calls for adopting multiple perspectives in an effort to better understand the entirety of complex public issues.

David Farmer opens the symposium with an analysis of Henry V and

Richard III. As Farmer notes, Shakespeare looks both outwards – to set-ting of the play, the structure of the play itself, and its larger social context – as well as inwards – to the motivations of and lessons learned by each character. Accordingly, Farmer's analysis operates on both levels. He looks inward, considering Henry and Richard's qualities as individuals and the leadership lessons that have been drawn from their examples. He also looks outward, exploring how the structure and poetry of Henry V communicates an understanding of the subtext and often hidden underpinnings of policy leadership.

Second, Catherine Horiuchi gives a powerful critique of the planning and implementation of the new eastern span of San Francisco's Bay Bridge. Her central point is that actions must speak louder than words – that the bridge itself must be stronger than the rhetoric surrounding it. The test of the new span will be its ability to deliver drivers safely and quickly across San Francisco Bay. However, words spread more widely than can a bridge roadbed. Press releases, news stories, opinion pieces and social media posts reach around the globe, vastly outstripping the bridge itself, which only reaches from Oakland to Yerba Buena Island. Critically, words spoken by policymakers, planners and budget appropriations committees overpower the silent and passive action of the bridge itself. Using King Lear as her lens on the project allows Horiuchi to contrast the rational and quantifiable action of the span against the qualitative and emotionally laden political discourse surrounding its planning and construction. Lear chooses to val-ue proclamations of familial love more highly than the loving actions of Cordelia, with disastrous consequences. Having linked real-world power to a display of language, Lear is surprised when competition moves from the rhetorical to the physical realm. So, too, Horiuchi contrasts the quantifiable behavior of a bridge with the value-laden and politically charged language that framed its planning and construction, giving a cautionary tale of the power of language to lead to unexpected consequences.

The final piece continues the exploration of language, power and the lim-itations of projecting idealized visions onto the real world. Wachhaus reads The Tempest as a laboratory for experimenting with sovereignty and the exercise of power. The island lies outside of the bounds of civilization, al-lowing the characters shipwrecked there to re-imagine social order. Lacking resources and practical knowledge of the island, their only tools (and base of power) are words. In this respect, The Tempest is the obverse of King Lear. Lear moves from demonstrated applied power and engaged gover-nance (a successful reign) to the less fixed realm of language. The Tempest meditates on the limitations of words and the difficulties of translating ideas into action. For Wachhaus, one of the central lessons of The Tempest is that social structure is inescapable. Even in the isolated and amorphous setting of the shipwreck island, we need to impose a social structure in order to make sense of the world around us. Wachhaus suggests that pursuing a collaborative approach, rather than attempting to impose a personal vision, may be more productive.

Shakespeare continues to hold appeal because of his ability to portray our inner workings – our passions, foibles, and dreams – as well as the complexity and depths of our social relations. Much as with public managers, Shakespeare's characters occupy complex worlds made up of competing agendas and deep social ties, and constrained by limitations on time, knowledge and resources. His characters endure not because complexity reduces them to functionaries but because constraints allow us to see more clearly the richness of their humanity. For public administration to remain meaningful, it must likewise adopt means of embracing its passions, foibles and dreams. Critically, it must also retain the ability to step back from the stage and view itself at a distance, to transcend the individual perception and take in the entirety of the play.

Source: Reprinted with permission from *Public Voices* journal, Marc Holzer, Editor in Chief, 2022.

Theatre productions have provided ample fodder for students of administration throughout the centuries, and now into the twenty-first. Those vignettes would be valuable to public administrators throughout their careers. The potential pool of adages and reflections is virtually limitless. Incorporating the humanities as requisite resources into public administration and public policy degree programs, as well as in-service training and certificates, would expose students to insights and critiques, likely triggering thoughtful reactions as they serendipitously and, perhaps uncomfortably, encounter such messages throughout their careers – at the movies, on the home screen, on their phones, on the stage, in engaging novels and even in the Sunday comics.

Some sustained scholarly efforts have sought to bring unorthodox resources to the attention of public administration scholars, instructors and students on an organized basis. Dwight Waldo, a pillar of the field of public administration, understood and advocated for integrating humanistic insights into the study of public administration. According to Brack Brown and Richard Stillman (1986):

> Waldo had a special interest in humanistic perspectives in public administration. His own work drew heavily upon history and philosophy. While at Berkeley he wrote a 157-page monograph with the title *The Novelist on Organization and Administration: An Inquiry into the Relationship between Two Worlds* (1968). (Brown and Stillman, 1986)

He described his interest in the novel and the novelist thus:

> When, in the forties, I turned first to the practice and then to the professional study
> of public administration, I turned also to the reading of "administrative novels" – as
> I have come to call them ... With the passage of time my interest in the administra-
> tive novel became what might be described as a hobby ... I became – and remain
> – convinced that from such novels one can learn a great deal of value, and learn it
> painlessly; and that practicing administrators and students of administration ought
> to be aware of and exploit this resource. (Waldo, 1968)

Waldo annotated scores of contemporary novels in *The Novelist on Organization and Administration* (1968). He identifies three types of fiction directly related to public administration. These include bureaucratic fiction, in which the plot is centered on bureaucratic relationships; administrative fiction, involving decision making within an organization; and political fiction, focusing on the difficulties and possibilities of the politics-administration continuum. Generally, Waldo finds a pessimistic view by scores of authors as to administration's impact on individual values. His commentary on *The Plague*, by Albert Camus, underscores the dark, but perhaps realistic, view of bureaucracy that is so often found in the humanities:

> Camus' portrait of bureaucracy in *The Plague* is an exceptionally hostile one. Some
> of his criticisms are familiar: the impersonality of the bureaucrat; his refusal to make
> human exceptions to the rule. ... What is novel is Camus' insistence that official-
> dom is irrelevant in times of crisis. When plague strikes ... the local public officials
> are overcome by inertia. Instead of acting immediately, they "send for instructions."
> When events force them to act, their response is halfhearted and ineffective ... As
> a stranger ... remarks: "What they're short on is imagination ..." (Waldo, 1968)

Following Waldo's leadership, for several decades some faculty concerned with the study of administration utilized one particular mode of humanistic commentary, the novel, as a supplement to social science texts. Inquiries into that relationship between entertainment and administrative elucidation, between humanity and social science, have identified many relevant novels beyond Waldo's compendium. The use of novels has also led to awareness, often more implicit than explicit, that fiction can be a more interest-evoking, and therefore a more effective entre and continuing impetus to administrative insights, than the orthodox material. The effectiveness of novels as part of the curriculum, however, is limited by their length and by the associated time required to read them in courses already heavy with texts and supplementary readings.

Beyond the novel, *Literature in Bureaucracy* (Holzer, Morris and Ludwin, 1979) offers an interdisciplinary collection of short stories, poetry and musical lyrics within a conceptual framework for exploring key issues in public administration ranging from power to corruption to human factors. That collection, and its associated pilot project funded by the National Endowment for the Humanities, clearly showed that using literature to teach public administration offers the following advantages. It:

- Overcomes the limitations imposed by the traditional texts and approaches, which can be dry and uninviting.
- Explores key administrative issues often overlooked in traditional texts, ranging from power conflicts to corruption to the pervasive influence of human factors.
- Draws together a continuum of administrative concerns into a single framework to better emphasize the interrelation of these concerns.
- Enables students to appreciate the drama and underlying complexity of administration, a quality more apparent in fiction than traditional texts.
- Introduces personal cases and inside perspectives on the ways that organizations actually function.
- Provides excellent transitional material for in-service students who are reconciling "real-world" experience with the academic study of administration.
- Provides the means for testing a number of interdisciplinary teaching models, involving both social science and humanities faculty.
- Helps to sharpen students' critical thinking about important administration issues.
- Encourages students to read literature and other outside material as an important source of information about administration.
- Is particularly appropriate in a curriculum of "relevant career education" such as public administration because it combines the practical understanding of administration with the traditional value of humanistic study: an insight into the individual and their place in the world.

Holzer, Morris and Ludwin draw upon several types of commentary through fiction, including the novel, to construct one particular conceptual framework – the Matrix of Concern – drawn from those works themselves (Table 2.1). Because the usefulness of fiction is often constrained by the lack of an organizing principle or sorting device, that framework should enhance fiction's administrative utility by providing a "handle." Others may disagree with the framework and interpretations of a specific work, but that disagreement should be the reason for reanalysis rather than for ignoring unorthodox commentaries. Although each work of fiction is classified by a primary emphasis, that classification should not be interpreted as precluding its relevance to other points in the framework. And as with more orthodox forms, this type of material should not be viewed primarily as a source of rules or proverbs, but merely as a stimulus to thought and action, as a type of devil's advocacy. Such works are

Table 2.1   *Matrix of concern in fiction*

	Not Bothered	Bothered, But Feeling Inadequate to Object	Bothered, But Coping through Pity or Scorn	Coping by Disassociating Oneself from the Organization
Intraorganizational				
a. Stifling				
to				
b. Corrupt				
	Pessimistic Warnings of Administration's Impacts on Individual Values			
Extraorganizational				
a. Impersonal				
to				
b. Unjust				

primarily critical as warnings or cautions, but some are even positive in terms of responses by public servants.

One dimension, representing relatively "independent" variables, seems to crystallize about either intraorganizational (interaction between bureaucrats) or extraorganizational (interaction between bureaucrats and clients) problems. "Dependent" variable concerns appear to be the individual's reaction to organizational pressures. Those reactions – by employee or client – can be arrayed along a continuum from "not bothered" through "bothered, but feeling inadequate to object" and then "bothered, but coping through pity or scorn" to "coping by disassociating oneself from the organization." The confluence of both dimensions appears as a predominantly pessimistic view of administration's impact on individual values, a warning that is not as apparent in the traditional social science literature, and that therefore deserves our attention.

Within each subcategory, it is further differentiated along the dependent dimension. The construction of that matrix should not, however, be mistaken for an argument that the administrative commentaries contained in fiction are narrowly conceived in two dimensions. We do not mean to imply that any one piece deals only with the concerns of a single category; indeed, almost all aspects of administration are reflected in fiction. Our discussion is only a means of identifying a structure by which we can initially simplify, and thereby encourage, a continuing administrative interest in the full range of complex humanistic commentary as addressed across the intra- and extraorganizational dimensions below (Holzer, Morris and Ludwin, 1979).

INTRAORGANIZATIONAL

Commentaries with intraorganizational foci suggest a subcontinuum of concern for an institution's impact on an individual's values, which ranges from "stifling" to "corrupting." Fiction often deals with the effects of organizational structure and pressures on employees and the various mechanisms that employees use – or do not use – to survive in an organization.

Stifling

The most consistent message contained in the humanities is probably that a bureaucratic environment has detrimental effects on an individual's sense of independence. The argument is clearly that the institutional environment is empty, insensitive, and therefore repressive. Workers may be stifled by their environment and feel that their freedom to think and act to the best of their ability is restricted by organizational policy or tactics. Some may suffer these limitations more severely, seeing their jobs as hopeless or useless, and may feel crushed or demoralized by the system, ceasing to function effectively at all.

The literary community is fond of reminding us that bureaucracy can also adversely affect bureaucrats. For instance, in *The Scarlet Letter* (1850 [1947]), Nathaniel Hawthorne's description of "The Custom House" forces the reader, through the author's role of detached insider, to recognize the encroaching listlessness of spirit, the sapping of intellectual vigor and individual initiative. Hawthorne suggests that the loss of "capability for self-support" affects every individual who comes to depend on the public payroll for financial security. His characters symbolize the debilitating effects of a government organization, resulting in an employee's lack of physical or mental vigor.

Overall, fictional public bureaucrats take a beating. Most writers confirm a pessimistic view of bureaucracy's impact on its clients and even its own employees. Even when we find positive images, they may be overwhelmed, as in the one passage in Steinbeck's *The Grapes of Wrath* (1939) which praises an effective federal bureaucracy for protecting its clients in a humane work camp; nevertheless, his overarching theme condemns corrupt local bureaucrats – police in league with banks to evict sharecroppers – and growers who exploit farm workers. Our society has been presented with, and has bought into, an image of public servants as uncaring and untrustworthy, entangled in red tape, failing to apply the common sense with which average citizens are endowed. The popular view of the public bureaucracy – created in part through the lens of fiction – is that it barely produces intended results, but is profuse in its production of negative and unethical behaviors – stifling, demoralizing, corrupting, impersonal and unjust.

As a generic icon in administration, public or private, is the typical organizational man who is no longer bothered by his plight, who has willingly bartered all sense of initiative, originality and risk for organizational security. In 1878 it was featured on stage in Gilbert and Sullivan's *H.M.S. Pinafore*, an operetta in which Sir Joseph Porter indicates that he rose through a hierarchy from office boy to the post of First Lord of the Admiralty:

> I never thought of thinking for myself at all.
> I thought so little they rewarded me
> By making me the Ruler of the Queen's Navee! (Gilbert and Sullivan, 1878 [1936])

That strategy for "promotion by blind devotion" is as apparent today in novels and movies with political, bureaucratic and military themes.

The deadening effects of organization are graphically revealed by such images as Charlie Chaplin's 1936 movie *Modern Times*, a well-known pictorial presentation of the man-as-machine theme that emphasizes the plight of workers as slaves to an assembly line. As a commentary directed toward the other, upper end of the hierarchy, W.H. Auden's poem "The Managers" suggests that those who staff the upper reaches of the hierarchy develop as much into unfeeling cogs in a machine as do their underlings (Auden, 1948 [1967]).

Although most intraorganizational commentaries portray the individual as passively, thoughtlessly acceding to the impact of the bureaucracy, some do suggest the second point in the dependent continuum of the matrix – that they are indeed bothered by their role, but feel inadequate to contest it. For instance, "The Perforated Spirit," the subject of a poem by Morris Bishop, resents being coded, punched and sorted by the personnel department, yet still acknowledges that they are the "masters of my fate" (Bishop, 1959). Mr. Zero, the appropriately named focal point of Elmer Rice's (1923 [1933]) play *The Adding Machine*, has at least a dull awareness that a quarter-century of routine drudgery has been futile, but nevertheless is willing to accede to it. George Orwell's (1950) British colonial officer resists *Shooting an Elephant* (a short story), but still feels compelled to do so by a mob. Or there is Flinders, a competent agricultural specialist, who feels incompetent in a bureaucratic setting, "The Meeting" (a scenario from Shirley Hazzard's (1968 [1988]) novel *People in Glass Houses*), but his reaction is to internalize his sense of inadequacy, not to rail against his dilemma.

Only far less frequently is the individual portrayed as having achieved the third type of reaction, as having developed a personally satisfying understanding which helps him resist organizationally induced insecurities. For instance, in *His Honor Claudius Watts*, the subject of a short story by Edmund G. Love,

a government clerk without a professional future fights bureaucratic anonymity by grasping authoritative titles in another organizational context, his
suburban community. Although he avoids the responsibilities attached to those
titles, conning another citizen into doing much of the work, that "dupe" is an
enviable figure insofar as he is more amused than enraged by the pompous
clerk he pities.

The most admirable individual reaction, rejection of a stifling environment,
is stressed in such short stories as "Deer in the Works" by Kurt Vonnegut,
Jr. (1955 [1985]). A small newspaper entrepreneur's plight as he trades his
intellectual freedom for the security of a large organization is reflected in
a deer trapped in a huge factory complex. But as he frees the deer, contrary to
orders, he simultaneously turns his back on the other organizational context,
his suburban community.

Corrupt

The continuum of concern (the dependent dimension of the matrix) which
we have applied to one part of the intraorganizational, stifling-corrupting
continuum, can also help clarify the message that individual progress in
a large organization is all too often at the expense of others. There are those
who react by perverting the goals of the organization, who use the forms and
the procedures of the system to achieve their own personal ends. Whether the
employees accept their plight quietly, rage against it impotently, adopt a stance
of pity or scorn, or finally leave the organization is often determined by the
kinds of pressures experienced and the nature of the characters themselves. In
this context, public managers should be concerned not only with what happens,
but also with why things happen and the ways they could possibly have been
avoided or rectified.

Robert Graves's (1917 [1955]) poem "Sergeant-Major Money," for
example, portrays the Sergeant Major as an "old stiff surviving" by habitually
impersonal actions. But Graves warns us that although most men might toler-
ate that stifling environment, others, severely affected but feeling helpless to
act within established organizational channels, may inadvertently be forced
to unintended, often immoral, reactions ranging from suicide and insanity to
murder. Similarly, James Thurber's (1942 [1980]) short story, *The Catbird
Seat*, is a farcical example of how aggressive, insensitive misuse of power is
itself "criminal." Thurber portrays an ambitious supervisor whose callousness
costs competent employees their jobs, but in the process induces equally irre-
sponsible reactions by one employee seeking to maintain his position.

The full range of concern for the individual is contained in any one of several
complex portrayals of moral lassitude. One of the most realistic is Heinar
Kipphardt's (1968) play, *In the Matter of J. Robert Oppenheimer*. Based on

the transcript of that atomic scientist's administrative trial for charges of being a security risk, several characters in the play epitomize the mindless bureaucrat whose capacity for "judgment" is constrained by a misplaced organizational loyalty. The author also suggests that even scientists can unthinkingly be immoral for their blind devotion to such projects as the A-bomb or H-bomb. Only one of Oppenheimer's judges is bothered by the matter before him, yet is timid in his objections and inadequate to stop the proceedings. Oppenheimer himself represents a range of concerns throughout his life, vacillating between extremes. At times he devoted himself to projects, such as the A-bomb, which deeply troubled his conscience. In other contexts, such as the H-bomb project, he is more likely to opt for moral integrity strained by a misplaced organizational loyalty. The author also suggests that even scientists can unthinkingly be immoral for their blind devotion to such projects.

Henrik Ibsen's play *An Enemy of the People* (1882 [1973]) powerfully approaches the theme of corrupt behavior, though in the looser organizational context of a political movement. Dr. Stockman, who initially expects to be lauded for discovering that the water supply is contaminated, is judged a danger to his town's economy and thereby socially ostracized. All too many of the townspeople blindly condemn him for the truth, and most of his former allies follow suit. Finally, the doctor's family and one ally choose isolation rather than contribute to the triumph of economic over moral rationality. Ibsen is clearly warning us that an organization's pressures for conformity are too often at odds with morality and truth.

Heller's (1961) *Catch-22* has lent its title to the English language as a condition we all fear: a bureaucratic system built on circular reasoning from which there is no escape. In *Catch-22*, a World War II bureaucratic farce which was presented first as a novel and then as a movie, corruption is prevalent, accountability nonexistent, and the treatment of individuals callous. The war's goals are replaced by those of profit and individual comfort. The interests of the illicit M&M Syndicate become more important than military success or soldiers' lives. Similarly, Colonel Cathcart continually increases the number of dangerous missions required by his men, solely for the purpose of enhancing his own reputation. Perhaps the most important theme in the movie, as in the novel, is the ludicrous nature of bureaucratic rules.

In Ken Kesey's (1962) classic *One Flew over the Cuckoo's Nest*, patient McMurphy disturbs the routine procedures of a mental hospital. Big Nurse and other staff serve the controlling needs of the "system." The staff is presented as callous and control oriented. Big Nurse, in particular, is the epitome of a narrow-minded functionary. The crux of the movie is that her authority is challenged by McMurphy's informal power. Her custodial assumptions are in direct conflict with a humanistic orientation toward patient/staff relations. Ultimately, Big Nurse and the organization triumph in the harshest terms, and

McMurphy's power is negated by subjecting him to the horrible consequences of an irreversible and unnecessary lobotomy – transforming a sane patient into a compliant vegetable.

EXTRAORGANIZATIONAL

Critiques involving the interaction of agency and client also seem to be bimodally differentiated. One focus is the argument that bureaucracy is too impersonal, too insensitive a vehicle for effective response to public demands. Anyone who has ever applied unsuccessfully for a permit or license, or who has been caught up in a complex legal or financial matter, or who has been the victim of a computer error, will readily empathize with characters caught up in similar situations. All too familiar are the inaccessibility and cold indifference of the officials, the non-committal jargon and the need to repeat requests endlessly to one clerk, then another, and another. The other focal point is the admonition that insensitivity easily shades into injustice. At what point bureaucracies cease to be impartial and start to become indifferent to the point of being unjust is often a fine line to discern. From the client's or public's point of view, bureaucracies are nearly always assumed to be insensitive and too cumbersome to accommodate any situation not covered by existing rules and regulations. Though the client's assertions may or may not be true in any given case, what is important for public administrators is to observe the tendencies of bureaucracies to establish self-perpetuating procedures that slight clients or treat them unjustly.

In contrast to intraorganizational analyses, such fiction-based commentaries seem more narrowly delineated insofar as they do not advance the theme of organizational rejection as a possible individual reaction (the fourth point on the continuum of concern). Rather, they consistently suggest that clients must somehow cope with the bureaucracy.

Impersonal

Administrative fiction often involves the extraorganizational interaction of agency and client, seeming to view the organization as either impersonal or unjust. Some view bureaucracy as ridiculously insensitive. In Zoschenko's (1963) *The Galosh*, the trivial task of recovering a lost boot becomes an overly formal run-around; by the time he recovers the boot, the other half of the pair has been lost. In Kishon's (1972) *The Jerusalem Golem*, a taxpayer whose name is identical to that of a harbor is inadvertently billed for the huge cost of its dredging; unable to get the computer to correct the error, he is also billed for payments toward a debt he cannot pay. In the end, the computer error is not only reversed, but becomes a monthly payment to him which the bureaucracy is just as unwilling and incapable of correcting in its favor.

A frequent theme is that the client is perturbed instead of passive, but still an inadequate force. In *Pigs Is Pigs* by Ellis Parker Butler (1905 [1949]), a mindless bureaucracy has complicated, rather than solved, relatively insignificant individual problems. In each case, however, the vehicle of satire and an outcome which is detrimental to the organization suggest the third type of concern, pity of the organization that substitutes for simple anger.

Unjust

The most important administrative critique contained in fiction may be that large organizations are so characteristically impersonal as to be unjust. *The Martyrdom of Peter Ohey*, by Slawomir Mrozek (1967), for instance, is a farcical play about passive obedience. Ohey exercises so much deference to authority, no matter how ludicrous the request, that he commits suicide to please the bureaucracy. Franz Kafka's (1925 [1956]) terrifying confrontation, *The Trial*, sometimes presented as a play, is perhaps the most widely recognized literary examination of the problem of the helpless individual enmeshed in a bureaucratic nightmare.

Ralph William's (1968) science fiction tale, "Business as usual during alterations," deals with an unusual dilemma confronting executives of a large department store. Should they take advantage of a mysterious machine which can duplicate anything? The senior of the two executives unthinkingly capitalizes on the invention, failing to recognize that its use will quickly contribute to the degeneration of society. The other objects, unsuccessfully, that a broader responsibility to humanity outweighs a narrower loyalty to the organization.

As social commentary, fiction typically pillories the bureaucracy, arguing that little people are oppressed by large organizations. Dickens's (1857) *Containing the Whole Science of Government* (*Little Dorrit*) warns us that insensitivity has serious consequences. "The Circumlocution Office" is a bureaucratic jungle that humiliates, frustrates, and overwhelms the individuals it was established to serve. Concerned more with its own perpetuation than with ministering to the public, the Office has become a "politico-diplomatic hocus pocus piece of machinery," the exemplification of "HOW NOT TO DO IT." Form and process have become ends in themselves rather than the means of providing services to the citizens, who suffer their absence. Similarly, Kosinski's (1975) *Cockpit* relates an incessant shuffling between offices to gain official recognition or authorization, and the special privileges of top-level bureaucrats; Kosinski portrays a government which, instead of serving its citizens, serves instead to victimize or even destroy them. And one of Tom Wolfe's (1987) themes in the best-selling *Bonfire of the Vanities* is the callous and unthinking behavior of criminal justice officials.

The power of fiction may be gauged by its influence on language. Perhaps Kafka is the most recognized critic of bureaucracy via fiction, even to the extent of the generally accepted adjective "Kafkaesque." He suggests that that "objective" rules may reduce individuals to objects, and bureaucrats may become inured to the public's pain. Some of the most depressing anti-client tales are Kafka's, such as *The Trial* (1925 [1956]), in which the character K. is the victim of a seemingly irrational, faceless organization. The novel is about how a little man, an ordinary middle-level bank manager, is suddenly arrested, tried and executed without any charge. Because the storytelling in the novel exists simultaneously both as a narrative and as an allegory, it is open to different readings by various people. It can be seen as a sociopolitical fable about a ubiquitous and omnipotent power machine, taking place in the real world and creating an atmosphere of alienation dubbed "Kafkaesque" ever after. Or it can be interpreted as a psychological and/or theological novel where a person is in perpetual trial for his/her sins, regardless of guilt. The frustration with bureaucracy in *The Trial* works not only on the narrative level, but on the visual level as well, as do many novels that become the basis for movies. In the cinema version, Orson Welles (1962) creates a depressing surrealistic world full of fear and shadows, where endless gloomy labyrinths and stacks of files on never-ending shelves are an organic part of the world, not an exception to it.

Due to censored social science and restricted political discourse, such works of fiction have played very important roles in shaping public perceptions and attitudes (Holzer and Gabrielian, 1998, 2000). Authors from Eastern Europe, in particular, have openly, or in a disguised form, criticized bureaucratic inefficiencies and political corruption in their novels, plays, posters and pamphlets, For example, administrative fiction has long been an element of Russian literature, very often the most influential critique aimed at ills of the society. Of all Russian writers, Nikolai Gogol is the one who is most obvious as a source for administrative commentary in Russian fiction. Although his works date back to the middle of the nineteenth century, the bureaucratic world Gogol depicts in his stories and plays is the familiar world of red tape, abusive clerks, impersonal and intimidating executives.

Gogol's (1836 [1961]) *The Inspector General* is a play based on a classic plot of mistaken identity. The corrupted officials of a provincial town expect an incognito government inspector from the capital, St. Petersburg. Because of their corrupt practices and dismal performance, they so dread the inspection that they mistake a young man with manners, who stays at the local inn and refuses to pay, for the expected inspector. This young man – Khlestakov – in reality is a penniless nonentity, who uses the opportunity and "borrows" money from the mayor, accepts the mayor's servile hospitality, takes bribes both from local bureaucrats and the local populace, flirts simultaneously with the mayor's wife and daughter, and narrowly escapes before being exposed. It is important to note that Khlestakov does not manipulate local officials to get what he wants (as a matter of fact, he wants nothing but a little money to pay for the inn and have a dinner), but is manipulated and elevated by them. Gogol's (1842 [1956]) *The Overcoat* is a sad story of a poor little clerk who longs for only one thing in his life: a new overcoat, which in his eyes will not only warm him up, but upgrade his status as well. When he is robbed of his coat, the hero dies from dread and cold.

The tradition of critical examination of bureaucracy in Russia was continued in the works of such famous writers as Chekhov and others. Chekhov's (1883 [2016]) *The Death of a Chinovnik*, for example, told the story of a little bureaucrat who sneezed at a superior in a theatre, and was so afraid of the imagined consequences that he died from fear and dread. The line of bureaucratic criticism became weaker, but did not die, after the Bolshevik Revolution in 1917. For example, Mayakovsky launched a savage attack on Soviet bureaucracy in his play *The Bedbug* (1929 [1966]), wherein a futuristic Communist bureaucracy was portrayed as having nothing human left to offer.

In an essay on "Literature and public administration ethics," Frank Marini (1992) supports the use of literature:

> By reading imaginative literature, public administration students may gain not only a knowledge of key issues for the field, but also an empathetic grasp or vicarious experience of these issues ... Literature helps us feel the dilemma of an administrator responsible for upholding policy while confronted with questions of compassion, exception, human considerations, and specific circumstances, the frustrations of someone caught in bureaucratic red tape. (Marini, 1992)

The messages in novels, stories, cinema, television and plays should not be dismissed just because they are predominantly negative. Fiction can play a role in changing expectations of performance in the public sector. Narratives of people in organizations – the stories people tell – are an important source of insight for our understanding of organizations and management theories (Hummel, 1991). Bureaucracy's critics – writers, as well as those in other, associated media: reporters, artists and directors – are a societal asset insofar as they have assumed the responsibility for persistently addressing the full and subtle range of ethical issues within public organizations. They are warning us that public bureaucracies are often dysfunctional; enervating and inefficient; the antithesis of creativity; cancers in our social fabric. Novelists and others portray the clean, well-lit buildings which house our bureaucracies as some of the most dangerous places in our society. And because entertainment is a palatable conveyor of criticism, the messages in novels (as well as cartoons, movies, and other forms of artistic expression) may be especially effective in generating a dialogue within a bureaucracy, or between bureaucrats and clients. The "foil" might be a novel, or a movie based upon a novel, which portrays government as corruptly suppressing the truth. A dialogue between bureaucrats, knowledgeable critics and citizens could illuminate the implicit solutions suggested by authors – problem-solving approaches which often puzzle the public sector and may account for its failure to respond to critics.

It is important to note that although public administration, or bureaucracy, is predominantly criticized by public administration's critics, the arts and humanities do offer powerful and positive messages about public service. In terms of novels, Friedsam (1954) "explored the depiction of bureaucrats as heroes in American literature" (Lee and Paddock, 2001) As with Waldo's work on novels as cited above, however, that book-length content is now more likely to be pedagoically effective on the screen. The media does offer positive perspectives that highlight the dedication and competence of public servants. The number of relevant movies, however, is a tiny fraction of the tens of thousands that comprise the cinematic universe according to research by Mordecai Lee and Susan Paddock (2001) who, working from the premise that it is relatively easy to find stereotypical and negative examples of public management, could identify only 20 positive depictions of civil servants who are truly heroic. Using somewhat broader criteria that include public management as well as public administration, and the investigative press and whistleblowers as well, and expanding the database to include television and streaming series, we have identified a few more gems. All offer positive depictions as opportunities for effective advocacy of public service.

Incorporating the Arts and Humanities into the Public Administration Classroom

Those images need to be incorporated into our pedagogy. Cinema, broadcast and streaming images offer faculty powerful opportunities to discuss vignettes that underscore the Matrix of Concern (above) and core subjects in the field. For example:

• *Parks and Recreation*, a streaming series, portrays Leslie Knope as a manager (later a member of the city council) in a local Parks and Recreation Department as a determined protagonist who pursues service improvements over the skepticism and obstructionism of her colleagues. They block her at every turn, but Knope persistently pursues the public interest, community input and the worth of the public sector as a service provider.
• *All the President's Men* – a book and then a movie – presents public service from two perspectives. "Deep Throat," who provides confidential

advice to *Washington Post* reporters Carl Bernstein and Bob Woodward, is a high-level FBI official risking his career to uncover corruption at the highest levels of government. Identified only many decades later, the FBI Assistant Director acted while most others merely observed. Another FBI official, "Joe," is equally courageous. "Public service" also characterizes news media and their reporters who seek to bring corruption and malfeasance to the attention of the public. The *Washington Post* received the 1973 Pulitzer Prize for Bernstein's and Woodward's investigation of the Watergate case.

- *Brubaker* is cinema as political drama, based on the career-ending efforts of a prison superintendent whose reforms embarrassed the Governor of Arkansas. In the movie, a newly appointed prison warden, Brubaker, goes undercover as a new inmate, experiences abuse first hand, then announces who he really is and begins a reform program. He uncovers murderous criminal behavior by the prison authorities, refuses to cover it up when he is promised funds for improvements, and is fired. Refusing to accede to an "ends justify the means," the movie highlights the high ethical standards that many public servants aspire to.

- *Star Wars* is the classic movie plot of good versus evil (as are its sequels). The forces of justice are represented by good bureaucrats, beginning with Luke Skywalker and extending to members of the Rebellion. The forces of evil are Darth Vader and his mindless minions. Han Solo, an entrepreneur interested only in money, acts on the side of truth, justice and public service at opportune times.

- *Stand and Deliver* takes advantage of the big screen to portray the teaching profession as an opportunity for committed idealists to deliver on the promise of public education as opportunity for all. Jaime Escalante is a math teacher who is intensely committed to helping his minority students advance. He succeeds in helping his students pass the Advanced Placement examination in calculus, although at the cost of his health. The Educational Testing Service, however, questions their unexpected success as unrealistic, suggesting cheating, and requires them to take the test over. Escalante leads them in a successful second round of testing, inspiring future classes of underprepared students to replicate those successes.

- *Thirteen Days* is the retelling of how President John F. Kennedy and an informal ExComm group of his "best and brightest" advisors headed off the Cuban Missile Crisis. Rather than an authoritarian's ego-driven, hardline pattern of decision making, Kennedy and members of the ExComm argued internally, resisted the strident views of some of their generals, negotiated, made the most of informal channels in negotiating with the Russians, and successfully stepped down the crisis. That peaceful resolution of a potentially catastrophic confrontation was one of the American public sector's finest hours.

- *To Kill a Mockingbird*, a visualization of one of Harper Lee's best-selling volume of the same title, is not just about tolerance and justice. The sheriff exercises administrative discretion to protect a neighbor who defended a child, and in the process takes the life of the perpetrator of a heinous crime. The sheriff is acting to head off a dangerous situation, thereby achieving a justifiable outcome.

- *The West Wing*, over the course of seven seasons, portrays a fictional President Bartlet as a chief executive who is civic-minded and set on doing the right things. Those accomplishments result from smart strategies, fact-based decisions, ethical propensities and adept politics. Although he and his like-minded staff often prevail, President Bartlet is burdened by self-doubt, a chronic illness and fractures in the nation's political climate. *The West Wing* presents a balanced perspective of competence vs. catastrophe, of high-minded ideals vs. incremental realism. In so doing, it paints a portrait of public service and policy management that is closer to reality than is evident in typically prescriptive textbooks in the field of public administration.

The field needs to deepen and enliven the teaching of public administration and management, particularly in terms of ethics, by immersing students in cases delivered as digital media on large and small screens. Novels may be too time consuming. Public administration insights delivered on the screen may be the most powerful and accessible mode for alerting future and present public servants to the full range of humanistic and sociological concerns, as well as issues of public policy and implementation. After all, students are increasingly screen oriented, spending hours each day on their computers, their smart phones, their smart TVs. Each technology is capable of accessing a century's production of movies and eight decades of dramatic or comedic series produced for television. Movies and television productions, including series such as *The West Wing* or *Parks and Recreation*, are valuable, but often overlooked, aspects of engaged learning for students, scholars and practitioners of public management.

Insights offered on the screen may endure with students more so than those offered in traditional publications. Practicing managers and pre-service students "who stand to benefit most from insights into the practice of public administration often find traditional textbooks unappealingly 'dry' and ignore them, with relief, once they complete a course or degree" (Holzer, Morris and Ludwin, 1979). On the other hand, a well-selected film or episode from a television series can connect a student with the human elements of public administration – the people they serve and communities they will shape; the intraorganizational ethical dilemmas they will encounter; the conflicts between appointed professional and elected officials; and the disparities between competency and posturing.

Such graphic cases can imprint lessons and dilemmas on the enduring, visual memories of students, following Howard McCurdy and Charles Goodsell's views that fictional or virtual experiences may be as vivid as encounters with real bureaucrats (Holley and Lutte, 1999).

"Screen cases" are often cited in a media review or a scholarly publication as a teaching and learning resource directly relevant to public and nonprofit administration in areas such as budgeting, human resources and ethics. Vignettes from the arts and humanities offer opportunities to enliven the curriculum and the classroom. Each provides a common basis for discussion by students from many career paths and cultural contexts worldwide, often underscoring common bureaucratic dilemmas or conflicts around the globe.

Selected scenes may be available for downloads from YouTube or via web links. A search on the topic "government whistle blowers," for example, brings up a CBS series, "Whistleblower," that underscores how such individuals often risk their own safety to right a wrong. The series

> Takes a thrilling look into the real-life David vs. Goliath stories of heroic people who put everything on the line in order to expose illegal and often dangerous wrongdoing when major corporations rip off U.S. taxpayers ... Each hour introduces cases in which ordinary people step up to do the extraordinary by risking their careers, their families and even their lives to ensure other are not harmed or killed by unchecked, unethical corporate greed. (paramountplus.com, 2022)

Classroom discussion of each screen case can be accompanied, as appropriate, by online synopses, newspaper reviews, magazine articles, or video web links. Each can link to scenes illustrative of a teaching focus relevant to a chapter's topic, as represented in core public administration textbooks, for example *Public Administration: An Introduction* (Holzer and Schwester, 2022).

Integrating screen cases with established, but often unexciting courses can help build effectively upon introductory and advanced course matter, inspire students to the deeper calling of public service, and enable students to appreciate and critique stereotypes of bureaucrats as simply rule bound. Overall, they may help foster a deeper perception of the field of public service and administration.

Pedagogically, screen cases, as well as other humanistic forms of expression, can help enhance public administration courses in several ways:

1.   As cross-cutting resources applicable to multiple courses that underscore the intersections inherent in public service delivery, such as the very popular *Parks and Recreation* streaming cable series:

> One of the strongest themes of the show relates to public versus private provision of services. Ron Swanson may be the director of the Parks Department, but he sees government as the problem; very much at odds with his sometimes deputy – the politically ambitious Knope – who sees it as a solution. She wants government to solve problems big and small. (Deitchman, 2014)

2.   As focal points for weekly assignments, challenging students to link the movie or television episode to a particular chapter. *Star Wars* provides an excellent opportunity for crossing the values and leadership bridges. The evil, bureaucratic Empire initially uses a mindless bureaucracy to its advantage. Under a Weberian model, its legions can be described as coldly efficient, its information networks pervasive, its technological achievements superior. The Rebellion, however, ultimately triumphs by being much less bureaucratic – more motivated and innovative. In both *Star Wars* (1977) and *Return of the Jedi* (1983) individual initiative and on-the-spot innovation defeat seemingly impervious forces. The Empire's bureaucrats are stereotypical ciphers, unable to think, to react, to adapt (Holzer and Slater, 1995).

3.   As discussion tools to help students confront the realities of decision making in terms of choices and consequences. *The Wire*, for example, draws an unmistakable line between the decisions that public administrators make and the lived experiences of their constituents:

> With ethnographic depth, [*The Wire*] shows the unintended consequences of apparently minor managerial decisions and how they spin out and merge with other equally "innocent" decisions to sustain the very institutional conditions being decided against. It shows trade governed by the structures of global capitalism, and the effects of this trade, with visceral detail. (Holt and Zundel, 2014)

4.   As a means of underscoring personal responsibility. Again, *The Wire* communicates that no choice is passive, particularly in public management. Each episode does well to remind us – faculty and students alike – that the outcomes of our decisions and actions always affect people. Holt and Zundel (2014) note that this show:

> stays with human beings and their affairs, demonstrating how television, in continually keeping open the question of meaning, can serve as a "cultural forum" for collective, ideological reflexivity (Newcomb and Hirsch, 1983). Through

this involved concern for human lives, the viewer becomes implicated and, in the absence of explicit explanations or definite conclusions, co-opted into an open sensemaking process. It is, we argue, this sense of drawn-out complicity with what it means to live in and with an economy and its underbelly that makes watching *The Wire* a compelling experience.

Each of *The Wire*'s five seasons takes a different point of view as to Baltimore's social landscape: the illegal drug trade; seaport economy and unions; city government and bureaucracy; the public school system; and the news media. Its fixed, revolving point of view on a singular subject presents a sort of visual case study, one with no shortage of lessons for students of public administration (Holzer and LaFrance, 2021).

5. As an opportunity for investigating systems, and their accompanying puzzles, challenges and injustices, there is *Erin Brockovich*. In her pursuit to bring down a corrupt, polluting power company, we see Brockovich navigate legal, regulatory and social barriers. One such scene features Brockovich verbally taking down the company's hotshot lawyers, illustrating the bias and discrimination that she routinely faces in her pursuit (Forbes and Smith, 2007).

6. As appreciation for the "street-level bureaucrat" – who is often characterized as a hero. Screen cases also venture within the classroom, in films like *Freedom Writers* or *Stand and Deliver*. In the latter (1988), Jamie Escalante exceeds his title as math teacher, acting more as the "teacher-hero," as typified by Sandford Borins (2011). Escalante:

> overcomes the skepticism of burned-out colleagues and the harassment of the disbelieving, bureaucratic Educational Testing Service (ETS), which, relying on flawed and biased computer "analysis," accuses his minority students of cheating. ETS bureaucrats force the teacher's entire class to repeat an advanced placement calculus test. Fortunately, the students succeed under even greater pressure, but only due to their teacher's David-like efforts in opposition to the bureaucratic Goliath. (Holzer and Slater, 1995)

Escalante demonstrates will and perseverance in the goal of solving complex bureaucratic issues and injustices. Set to become public decision-makers, it is critical that students bear an understanding of their capacity for constituent service. If Escalante can elevate his students despite structures designed to reject that very action, what other barriers can be overcome? This is a case for vision and for perception, and perhaps as in Erin Brockovich, a motif central to the education of public administrators.

7. As templates for group discussion of a topic such as organizational dehumanization. For example, in the classic movie *Modern Times* (1936), Charlie Chaplin's enduring images of being subject to a "feeding

machine" and "caught in the gears" epitomize machine over man. Chaplin bounds from factory to prison to unionization effort – organizations of all kinds – without ever "[referring] to any enemy to be denounced, mocked or countered"; and still, this experience "does not result in any changes to the rules in favour of the worker" (Debenedetti, Huault and Perret, 2015).

8. As a lead into contemporary events from a historical perspective, comparing public administration perspectives from distinctly different societies. Vatche Gabrielian's (2000) analysis of "The rise and fall of the Soviet screen bureaucrat" presents role models and stereotypes that, in a silent movie, might well be mistaken for officials in the American or European contexts. In *Invictus* (2009), Nelson Mandela faces enormous social challenges in a post-apartheid South Africa; Bruce Baum (2010) reviews Mandela's leadership technique and "truth and reconciliation" approach to solving large-scale issues. And in Buchichio's *Behind the Truth* (*Detras de la Verdad*) (2014), two Uruguayan journalists are led by a whistle-blower through the ranks of his organization, filled with roadblocks endemic to organizations across societies.

9. As awareness that many relevant movies reinforce negative perceptions of government, communicating a skeptical or jaundiced view of "bureaucratic" public organizations and of their "bureaucrats." No media are more powerful than cinema or television, and on-screen images of bureaucrats are almost always negative, feeding on stereotypes of the "bumbling bureaucrat." In *Ghostbusters* (Reitman, 1984), which underscores the popular image of "bureaucrat as buffoon," an official of the Environmental Protection Administration (EPA) obnoxiously demands to inspect a storage facility for ghostly spirits. Rejected because he did not use the magic word "please," he returns with a court order. Told that his actions would surely endanger the populace, he arbitrarily and reflexively opts for rules and regulations, ordering the facility to be shut down. Even as his actions almost lead to disaster, the agitated bureaucrat still clings to the letter of the law. He is finally removed by the mayor, who opts for live, grateful voters over mindless bureaucrats and their rigid procedures. The enduring message is that bureaucrats are dangerously incompetent (Holzer and Slater, 1995).

10. As appreciation for a sense of social injustice and implicit agendas for social reform, implementing an assumed responsibility to frame the impact that such public servants can have on society:
    *   calling to account dysfunctional behaviour by leaders and bureaucrats.
    *   portraying the triumph of the good bureaucrat or leader over the bad counterpart.
    *   dramatizing profiles of very dedicated, very competent public servants.

How many dedicated, but often frustrated, Leslie Knopes (*Parks & Recreation*), Josh Lymans (*West Wing*), or Cedric Daniels (*The Wire*) are sitting in our classrooms? Or perhaps a Jim Harper (*The Newsroom*), Jaime Escalante (*Stand and Deliver*), Erin Brockovich (*Erin Brockovich*) or Erin Gruwell (*Freedom Writers*). Screen resources may help students envision themselves in the context of larger-than-life screen heroes, tapping into their inspirations, and leading them to develop their own narratives.

Despite an awareness of the utility of unorthodox media, analytical efforts oriented to fiction are constrained by a relatively narrow interest in the novel, most evident in Waldo's work. Howard McCurdy's "Fiction, phenomenology, and public administration" (1973) began to build momentum for an artistic-humanistic approach. McCurdy, for instance, presciently advised five decades ago that "the discipline has delineated too narrowly the variety of fiction that may be relevant to the teaching of administration." Fortunately, we now have a relative wealth of published commentaries that identify a wide range of artistic and humanistic teaching and learning resources.

In 1987, Lawrence L. Downey noted that fiction can explore conflicts in three predominant areas: legitimization of authority (e.g., *The Caine Mutiny*); the relationship of organizations to their external environment (e.g., *Agnes of God*); and the relationship of organizations to their internal environment (e.g., *An Officer and a Gentleman*). David A. Gugin (1987) expanded on the conflictual issue, focusing on fictional treatments of morality and ethics. He places these subjects in two general categories: external and internal. The external category deals with accountability and responsiveness to intent or traditional norms, while the internal subgroup is concerned with individual ethics or morals in conflict with organizationally demanded behavior. In 1995, Charles T. Goodsell and Nancy Murray published *Public Administration Illuminated and Inspired by the Arts*, examining film, poetry novels and aesthetic teachings for the study of such diverse topics as leadership, ethics and policymaking.

Artistic and humanistic perspectives have been further developed since the 1990s via the journal *Public Voices*, delving into artistic, historical, humanistic and reflective expressions relevant to the field of public administration. From the first issue highlighting Norman Rockwell's (1943 [1993]) iconic image of "Freedom of speech," *Public Voices* has featured cover art as stand-alone commentaries on the accomplishments and dysfunctions of public organizations. Insights flowing from *Public Voices* have offered a rich dialogue across enduring concerns in public administration:

• Bureaucratic stereotypes, positive as well as negative.
• Decision-making from the perspective of moral dilemmas.
• Management models that are drawn from the humanities, not just the social sciences.

Table 2.2   *Categorizing management fables*

	Personal growth of protagonist	Personal decline of protagonist
Organizational renewal	Heroic	Sacrificial Retributive
Organizational decline	Ironic	Tragic Satirical

- Leadership tensions between simplicity and complexity.
- Ethics and the moral strictures that guide the work of public servants.
- Symbolic architecture, including monuments, inscriptions, memorials and imposing buildings.
- Public service as a high calling for contributing to the health of our civic societies.
- Public-private clashes of core priorities.
- Public values, such as expectations that our public servants and governments will be honest and free from corruption.

Those insights have been drawn from a surprisingly broad array of critical observations beyond the social sciences. Novels are often cited, and *Public Voices* has extended fiction-based administrative analyses to movies and televised or streaming series. Short stories have long offered relatively compact administrative insights as fictionalized case studies, and commentaries in the journal have highlighted historical and science fiction, as well as many real-life case studies, as teaching resources.

Within and beyond *Public Voices* the interpretive power of the humanities has been explored by Sandford Borins, beginning with Governing Fables: Learning from Public Sector Narratives (2011) According to Borins in the chapter titled "Front-Line Innovators: Transformational Teachers in America":

> *Governing Fables* develops a four-quadrant matrix for classifying narratives, based on the plot trajectories for protagonists and for their organizational or societal context. In the heroic fable (upper left quadrant), a leader enables an organization to overcome a challenge and thereby renew itself and is rewarded both intrinsically and extrinsically. The opposite of the heroic fable is the tragic or satirical fable (lower right quadrant), in which the organization declines as a result of the failings of its leader or leaders. The ironic fable concerns a protagonist enriching himself in the context of organizational decline (lower left quadrant). An example is the kleptocrat who exploits his position of public leadership. The sacrificial fable (upper right quadrant) involves organizational renewal due to action by a protagonist that leads to his or her decline or even demise. The book classified the texts in terms of these fables and, for both countries, discussed the significance of the patterns by which texts populated the matrix. (Borins, 2012)

Borins goes on to offer that:

> Instructors frequently use short clips from moving-image texts (mainly film or television series) to illustrate management concepts or skills. (2011)

It follows that unorthodox critiques can be interpreted as complements, as well as interest-evoking supplements, to established theory. Such an interpretation seems valid if we concede that the humanities develop insights into real-world problems, insights founded in life experience rather than just intuition, with which academically oriented administrative theorists are not equally concerned. Those insights are not developed to fit into an established set of administrative concepts. It may, then, be worthwhile to clarify humanistic messaging via a conceptual framework as a means of crystallizing and highlighting those concerns, of identifying their own particular contributions to administrative analysis.

Government too often fails to untangle red tape, to eliminate waste, to treat its clients and employees humanely. From the perspectives of the public and their surrogates, avoidable human tragedies are all too routine. Messages that bureaucracy stifles productivity cannot be dismissed as simplistic, for many social science theories are grounded in the same assumptions. The same tensions that authors and artists underscore – bureaucratic control versus individual initiative – have been resurfacing for decades. They have staying power because the problems of bureaucracy are still unsolved, because the organizational sciences have not been able to change most organizations, because bureaucracy is still perceived as violating the public trust. Novels, short stories, movies and screen series offer as yet unexploited means for drawing attention to our most basic organizational concerns, and sometimes they underscore the same models that students of government also recommend.

TAKEAWAYS

- Public administration organizations provide for the collective wellbeing by implementing their government's promises.
- To deliver necessary public services, public servants have sworn to answer the call to serve their fellows and families.
- Unorthodox administrative commentaries can alert public administrators to problems that traditional scholarship is missing or minimizing: stifling environments, corrupting behaviors, impersonal encounters and unjust actions.
- Movies and streaming series are especially powerful commentaries and can enrich the curriculum.

- The arts and humanities also offer positive, powerful messages about public service.

SELECTIONS FOR FURTHER READING AND RESEARCH

Borins, S. (2011) *Governing Fables: Learning from Public Sector Narratives.* Charlotte, NC: Information Age Publishing. https://www.infoagepub.com/products/Governing -Fables

A welcome perspective that argues for the power of narratives and the skills necessary for adding such techniques to the public manager's set of competencies.

Goodsell, C. and Murray, N. (1995) *Public Administration Illuminated and Inspired by the Arts.* Westport, CT: Praeger Publishing.

An especially broad interpretation of public administration across disciplines and cultures that underscores the influence of unorthodox influences on public policy and administration.

Hummel, R. (2007) *The Bureaucratic Experience.* Fifth edition. New York: St. Martin's Press.

This volume is realistic in arguing that bureaucracy will always endure as a necessary organizational device, and this its dysfunctional consequences will endure as well despite our best efforts to the contrary.

Lynn, J. and Jay, A. (1989) *The Complete Yes Minister: The Diaries of a Cabinet Minister.* London: BBC Books.

A humorous window into political-administrative relationships, this most popular series exposes the less-than-professional tactics and human vulnerabilities of bureaucrats and politicians.

Public Voices Journal of the Section on Historical, Artistic and Reflective Expression (SHARE) of the American Society for Public Administration. https://www .publicvoices.us

An enduring dialogue of insights into public administration from salient and fresh perspectives.

REFERENCES

Alvarez, C., Casanova, G., Fau, H.C, López, N. and Álvarez, C. (Producers), and Buchichio, E. (Director) (2014) *Behind the Truth* [Motion picture]. Uruguay: Lavoragine Films.

American Society for Public Administration (2022) Code of Ethics Retrieved August 6, 2022, from https://www.aspanet.org/ASPA/Code-of-Ethics/Code-of-Ethics.aspx

Auden, W.H. (1967) *Collected Shorter Poems, 1927–1957.* New York: Random House.

Baum, B. (2010, December) Hollywood on race in the age of Obama: Invictus, Precious, and Avatar. *New Political Science*, 32(4).

Bishop, M. (1959) The perforated spirit. In Cole, W. (ed.), *The Fireside Book of Humorous Poetry*. New York: Simon and Schuster.

Borins, S.F. (2011) *Governing Fables: Learning from Public Sector Narratives*. Charlotte, NC: Information Age Publishing.

Borins, Sandford (2012, March) New development: Macroeconomic fables. *Public Money and Management*.

Brown, B. and Stillman, R.J. II. (1986) *A Search for Public Administration: The Ideas and Career of Dwight Waldo*. College Station, TX: Texas A&M University Press.

Butler, E.P. (1949) *Pigs Is Pigs*. London: St. Hugh's Press.

Chaplin, C. (1936) *Modern Times* [Motion picture]. USA: United Artists.

Chekhov, A.P. (2016) *Death of a Civil Servant*. Richmond: Alma Classics.

Debenedetti, S., Huault, I. and Perret, V. (2015, June) Resisting the power of organizations in modern times: May we all be Charlot? In XXIVème conférence annuelle de l'Association Internationale de Management Stratégique (AIMS 2015).

Deitchman, B. (2014) Public administration as must-see TV: "Parks and Recreation" in a world of public values and public interest. *PA Times*. https://patimes.org/public-administration-tv-parks-recreation-world-public-values-public-interest/

Dickens, C. (1857) *Little Dorrit*. London: Bradbury and Evans.

Downey, L. (1987) The use of selected fiction in teaching public administration. Paper presented at the first national conference on Public Administration, the Arts, and the Humanities, the New School for Social Research.

Eastwood, C. (2009) *Invictus* [Motion picture]. USA: Warner Bros.

Forbes, J.B. and Smith, J.E. (2007) The potential of Erin Brockovich to introduce organizational behaviour topics. *Teaching and Learning*, 4(3).

Friedsam, H.J. (1954, March) Bureaucrats as heroes. *Social Forces*, 32(3).

Gabrielian, V. (2000) The rise and fall of the Soviet screen bureaucrat. *Public Voices*, 4(2), 71–83.

Gilbert, W. and Sullivan, A.S. (1936) *H.M.S. Pinafore*. New York: Modern Library.

Gogol, N.V. (1956) *The Overcoat*. London: Merlin Press.

Gogol, N.V. (1961) *The Government Inspector*. London: Heinemann.

Goodsell, C.T. and Murray, N. (1995) *Public Administration Illuminated and Inspired by the Arts*. Westport, CT: Praeger.

Graves, R. (1955) Sergeant-Major Money. In *Collected Poems, 1955*. Garden City, NY: Doubleday.

Gugin, D.A. (1987) Bureaucratic decision making and bureaucratic ethics: an argument for the novel. Paper presented at the annual meeting of the American Society for Public Administration, Boston.

Hawthorne, N. (1947) *The Scarlet Letter*. New York: Holt, Rinehart and Winston.

Hazzard, S. (1988) *People in Glass Houses*. New York: Penguin Books.

Heller, J. (1961) *Catch-22*. New York: Simon and Schuster.

Holley, L. and Lutte, R.K. (1999) Public administration at the movies. *Public Voices*, 4(2).

Holt, R. and Zundel, M. (2014, October) Understanding management trade, and society through fiction: Lessons from "The Wire." *The Academy of Management Review*, 39(4), 576–85.

Holzer, M. and Gabrielian, V. (1998) Administrative fiction. In *International Encyclopedia of Public Policy and Administration*. New York and Denver, CO: Westview Press.

Holzer, M. and Gabrielian, V. (eds) (2000) *Bureaucracy on the Silver Screen: A World-wide Perspective*. Burke, VA: Chatelaine Press.

Holzer, M. and LaFrance, J. (2021) *Public Administration on the Screen*. Boston, MA: Institute for Public Service, Suffolk University.

Holzer, M. and Schwester, R. (2022) *Public Administration: An Introduction*. Third edition. Routledge: New York and London.

Holzer, M. and Slater, L.G. (1995) Insight into bureaucracy from film: Visualizing stereotypes. In Goodsell, C.T. and Murray, N. (eds), *Public Administration Illuminated and Inspired by the Arts*. Westport, CT: Praeger.

Holzer, M., Morris, K. and Ludwin, W. (1979) *Literature in Bureaucracy: Readings in Administrative Fiction*. Wayne, NJ: Avery Publishing Group.

Hummel, R.P. (1991) Stories managers tell: Why they are as valid as science. *Public Administration Review*, 51(1), 31–41.

Ibsen, H. (1973) *Eleven Plays of Henrik Ibsen*. New York: The Modern library.

Kafka, F. (1956) *The Trial*. New York: Modern Library.

Kazanjian, H (Producer), and Marquand, R. (Director) (1983) *Star Wars: Episode VI – Return of the Jedi* [Motion picture]. USA: Twentieth Century-Fox.

Kesey, K. (1962) *One Flew over the Cuckoo's Nest*. New York: New American Library.

Kipphardt, H. (1968) *In the Matter of J. Robert Oppenheimer: A Play Freely Adapted, on the Basis of the Documents*. New York: Hill and Wang.

Kishon, E. (1972) The Jerusalem Golem. In Kishon, E. and Goldman, Y. (eds), *Blow Softly in Jericho*. London: Deutsch.

Kosinski, J.N. (1975) *Cockpit*. New York: Bantam Books.

Lee, M. and Paddock, S. (2001) Strange but true tales from Hollywood: The bureaucrat as movie hero. *Public Administration & Management: An Interactive Journal*, 6(4).

Lucas, G. (1977) *Star Wars Episode IV: A New Hope* [Motion picture]. USA: Twentieth Century-Fox.

Marini, F. (1992, June 1) Literature and public administration ethics. *The American Review of Public Administration*, 22(2), 111–25.

Mayakovsky, V. (1966) *The Bedbug; [a play] and Selected Poetry. Klop, stikhi, noemy*. New York: Meridian Books.

McCurdy, H.E. (1973, January 1) Fiction phenomenology, and public administration. *Public Administration Review*, 33(1), 52–60.

Mrozek, S. (1967) *Six Plays*. Translated by Nicholas Bethell. New York: Grove Press.

Musca, T. (Producer), and Menendez, R. (Director) (1988) *Stand and Deliver* [Motion picture]. USA: Warner Bros.

NEA (National Education Association) (2020) Code of ethics for educators. Retrieved August 6, 2022, from https://www.nea.org/resource-library/code-ethics-educators

Newcomb, H.M. and Hirsch, P.M. (1983) Television as a cultural forum: Implications for research. *Quarterly Review of Film and Video*, 8(3), 45–55.

Oath of Office (2020) International Association of Chiefs of Police (IACP). https://www.theiacp.org/resources/resolution/law-enforcement-oath-of-honor

Orwell, G. (1950) *Shooting an Elephant and Other Essays*. New York: Harcourt, Brace & World.

Reitman, I. (1984) *Ghostbusters* [Motion picture]. USA: Columbia Pictures.

Rice, E. (1933) *Plays of Elmer Rice*. London: V. Gollancz.

Rockwell, N. (1943) Freedom of speech [Painting]. In *Public Voices*, 1(1), Fall, 1993. https://www.publicvoices.us/_files/ugd/d3a2e5_2c447ffa31ab418aaa11bcaba956e143.pdf

Salkind, A. (Producer), and Welles, O. (Director) (1962) *The Trial* [Motion picture]. USA: Astor Pictures Corporation.

Steinbeck, J. (1939) *The Grapes of Wrath*. New York: Viking Press.

The Athenian Oath (n.d.) PAIA Insider. https://paiainsider.syr.edu/another-beautiful -page/

Thurber, J. (1980) *The Thurber Carnival*. Franklin Center, PA: Franklin Library.

Vonnegut, K. (1985) Deer in the works. In *Welcome to the Monkey House: A Collection of Short Works*. New York: Dell.

Wachhaus, A. (2015) Symposium introduction: Bureaucracy and the Bard. *Public Voices*, 14(2), 5–7.

Waldo, D. (1968) The Novelist on Organization and Administration: An Inquiry into the Relationship between Two Worlds. Berkeley, CA: Institute of Governmental Studies, University of California.

Williams, R. (1968) Business as usual during alterations. In D. Knight (ed.), *One Hundred Years of Science Fiction*. New York: Simon and Schuster.

Wolfe, T. (1987) *The Bonfire of the Vanities*. New York: Farrar, Straus, Giroux.

Zoshchenko, M. (2009) *The Galosh: And Other Stories*. New York: Harry N. Abrams.

3. Delivering performance, as promised

IN PURSUIT OF TRUST

For more than a century the rigorous study of public administration has been improving government's capacities to produce services. There are now hundreds of public administration and public management programs, generally entitled Master of Public Administration (MPA), in the US, and several times that number globally. Their missions are to build capacity for the delivery of services to the public, and indeed they have fulfilled their promises by emphasizing economy, efficiency, effectiveness and equity. The top-rated MPA program at the Maxwell School of Citizenship and Public Affairs, for instance (Maxwell School):

> Seeks to enhance knowledge and develop skills essential to careers in public service. We believe public service means using one's abilities and opportunities to contribute to the broad public good across levels of government and with nonprofit and for-profit organizations ... The M.P.A. program is grounded in a comprehensive view of public service education that appreciates the need for three areas of mastery: formulating, implementing and evaluating policy; leading and managing organizations with diverse stakeholders; and applying rigorous and evidence-based analysis to inform decision making.

Despite having built a significant field of academic study, and despite having applied research findings to the solution of public problems, the conundrum is that for at least 50 years the public's perception of government's efficacy has been declining. That mismatch between increased competency and decreased trust should be received as a loud alert, a call for action. The field of public administration has missed opportunities to rebuild trust in government, to convince the public that government *is* doing a good job delivering on its promises, and to put forth a set of compelling arguments for the worth of public services.

Fortunately, one strategic and comprehensive approach, developed concurrently over the past five decades, offers the potential to reverse that lack of confidence. Performance improvement, grounded in the awareness that a productive society is dependent upon high-performing government, is the focal point that the public sector requires if it is to rebuild the public's trust, and therefore the willingess of the public and the business community to invest tax dollars.

Public performance matters because government plays a pervasive role in our personal lives and the health of our nations. The Secretary General of The Commonwealth Organization, the Rt. Hon. Patricia Scotland, made that argument persuasively to the Commonwealth Heads of Government Meeting (CHOGM) in July of 2022:

> The Commonwealth (54 countries) is here to walk with those who have put their faith clearly on the path for maintaining good governance. If you look at the Singapore-based Chandler Institute of Governance recently released Good Government Index, in Africa the majority of countries that are members of our Commonwealth are in the first or second tiers. What is it about them that enables them to govern more robustly?
>
> The Commonwealth has had a history of giving technical assistance. We have just concluded training 2000 senior government officials on the performance management principles of good governance, and we have created a system capable of being shared across all fifty-four countries: the Generally Accepted Performance Principles, or G.A.P.P.
>
> Just like accountancy principles, it enables you to objectively assess the quality and nature of the delivery of good governance. We hope this will be an objective guide to assist Commonwealth countries doing that which they should properly do to deliver good governance.
>
> For so many of us, the assessment of government performance is either good, bad or ugly – but it is a subjective, as opposed to an objective, analysis. What the Commonwealth Secretariat has just delivered is a way in which we can objectively assess how well our countries are doing and assist them to do better.
>
> The tragedy in our world is that there is not one country I can think of who can honestly say they are without error, in need of improvement or opportunities to change. So what our Commonwealth is doing is coming together, looking at what works, looking at what doesn't work, and helping us to strengthen us all.
>
> ("CHOGM Opening Ceremony," transcribed from publicly available video, September 20, 2022)

Earlier in the twenty-first century the Alfred P. Sloan Foundation in the US convened a group of experts to develop a set of principles for building public performance capacities; the effort concluded that building continuous improvement capacities offers government and nonprofit organizations an array of opportunities (Holzer et al., 2011):

- To inform government policy and management practices that can lead to performance improvements and policy developments, resulting in better practice and alignment of governmental services to community needs.
- To provide data that enables accountability and transparency.
- To enable informed communication between citizens, government and nonprofits so as to foster trust.

As a key element of performance improvement, performance measurement is an evidence-based tool that informs decision making at all levels and by all stakeholders. It encourages continuous service improvement and organizational learning to make services more efficient and effective. A performance measurement system is characterized by indicators permeating the mission, the strategic plan, the budget and day-to-day operations:

- A performance measurement system's indicators are commitments to what an organization values, what it aspires or promises to achieve in the near term and long term.
- An effective performance measurement system is reliable and valid so as to positively impact decisions ranging from policymaking through resource allocation to implementation.
- A performance measurement system must enable government and nonprofits to advance the interests and values of their stakeholders, including citizens, only to the extent that all stakeholders have opportunities for input into the system.
- A performance measurement system helps government and nonprofits add value to the lives of citizens.

In terms of accountability, performance measurement enhances accountability if the information collected, utilized and reported is not only accurate, but also clear, available and relevant at every level of decision-making and to all stakeholders. As such, the reported data must strike an appropriate balance between being comprehensible to stakeholders and useful to decision-makers and managers.

- Accountability includes, but is not limited to, reporting. Reporting should encourage and enable managers to use stakeholder feedback so that program modifications and adjustments are possible. Reporting should also enable stakeholders to understand how actual performance significantly differs from expected performance.
- Accountability implies that performance measurement data must be fit for use in decision making in terms of quality, detail and timeliness; measurement must capture geographic and demographic nuances.
- Accountability implies that data are subject to independent review.
- Accountability means that disaggregated data must address the interests of different audiences via performance reports.

In terms of the core dimension of trust that is prerequisite to support for government, performance measurement and reporting, by enhancing transparency and participation, augments the level of trust that stakeholders have toward their governments and nonprofits. As such, performance measurement that is accessible to citizens helps to generate a more trusting relationship between citizens and governments or their nonprofit agents:

- Trust and accountability are linked when the specific informational needs of different stakeholders are satisfied.
- Trust in government and nonprofits on the part of citizens is built when citizens are given opportunities to listen, ask questions, and provide meaningful input toward both the data to be produced and the performance measures to be used.
- Trust in citizens on the part of government and nonprofit managers is built when citizens take an active role in utilizing data to assess and improve government and nonprofit performance.
- A performance measurement system's indicators are commitments to what an organization values, what it aspires or promises to achieve in the near term and long term.

WHO OR WHAT IS A "STAKEHOLDER"?

Broadly defined, "stakeholder" is a term meant to represent every person, group or organization that has a direct or indirect interest in the activity, the agency or the program. Stakeholder is perhaps the most commonly used word to describe the "who" of an organization, perhaps because it is often the most broadly defined, such as Edward R. Freeman's (1984), "Any group or individual who can affect or is affected by the achievement of the organization's objective."

The reality, however, is much more nuanced if performance improvement is to be achieved on a long-term basis. Doing so requires a sensitivity to many constituencies, an awareness of opportunities to develop partnerships, and a realization that multiple participants are relevant. Potential stakeholders may include, but are not limited to:

- Voters
- Customers
- Communities
- Citizens
- Employees
- Board members
- Businesses and their representatives
- Other units of government: local, state/provincial, national, international
- Funding agencies
- Partners organizations: public, nonprofit, private
- Unions or professional associations

- Foundations, charities and informal groups
- Community organizations
- The media.

Some definitions of stakeholders may be ambiguous. "Community" is often defined as simply a group of people living in the same place or having some common characteristics. For government, however, the community is exceptionally broad. The community served by government is typically a large collection of different groups which include both people and organizations. Should the government be conscious and sensitive to the business community? Certainly. Most of the time the operations of an agency or program will have an impact on both people and business, and most of the time people and business have a close mutual connection with one another. But sometimes governmental or pseudo-governmental programs serve more of a niche community. The homeless, the aged or students are just a few communities which are often mentioned. The definition of community will reflect an agency's specific operations.

A trend in recent years has been one of government shifting toward a more "customer-focused" approach to governance. What do we mean by "customer-focused" governance? Well, just as a business provides goods and services to its customers, in many ways so too does the government. For example, roads might be considered both a good and a service. The road itself is a tangible product produced by or on behalf of the government which provides the service of transportation facilitation. Let's say, for example, that the roads in a particular area are in a state of disrepair. This can be both frustrating and costly for the users of those roads. This frustration will most likely be pointed toward those who are in charge of maintaining the roads (i.e., the government).

If a government does not view the road users as customers, it may disregard these frustrations and chalk it up to providing the best services for the money available. If, on the other hand, the government does view road users as customers, it will recognize that alienating its customer base will result in a loss of institutional credibility, erosion of voter support, and perhaps even a reduced willingness to provide the government with the funds it needs to make the necessary road improvements.

Viewing citizens as customers creates a two-way relationship between the government and citizens, which is quite different from top-down philosophies and practices. An example of this is drawn from the state of Colorado which reformed their performance management system to reflect a "customer-focused" model. This customer focus provided the basis for their entire performance framework. But exactly what do they mean by the term customer? To clarify, the official statements from the state posited that:

> We are changing the way government does business in Colorado – we don't serve faceless taxpayers, we serve customers. We encourage government agencies to integrate the following principles of a customer-focused culture in their respective organizations:
> - Every employee serves at least one direct customer, internally and externally
> - A customer-focused culture views the customer journey as a singular, critical experience rather than a set of disconnected touch points
> - Customer satisfaction is fundamental to true customer service; customer surveys and focus groups are fundamental to understanding how we can better improve our processes (Scheminske, 2015)

Not only were the citizens being served viewed as customers, but potentially those working in government viewed each other as customers. If a department was tasked with issuing a report to another department, the department requesting the report could be viewed as the customer. In this way, feedback was a continuous and multi-directional dialogue.

"Internal" and "external" stakeholders are also imprecise, but common, terms. Sharma's (2008) "6 principles of stakeholder analysis" characterizes internal stakeholders as those people and programs that work closely with the agency, beginning with the leadership within a program. Being accountable to those within the organization is a primary feature of a high-performance organization. Accountability requires good communication, and if staff are aware and considerate of internal stakeholders, they are on the way to good internal communication.

The leadership and management teams are not the only internal stakeholders. Everyone working on or around the project should be considered in the planning phases. Individuals at all levels of the organization will have an impact on the project, particularly those who are relied upon to complete project objectives or to provide project support.

Other agencies can often be considered internal stakeholders as well. For example, many public organizations rely on a central purchasing department for everything from capital equipment to office supplies. These departments can play a crucial role in the success of a program and should be considered and consulted early on. The growth in contracting out makes this topic of particular importance to many organizations. The risks are in not properly managing and engaging internal stakeholders in the context of contracting out.

External stakeholders may be easier to conceptualize. These are the people, groups and organizations that exist outside of the organization, yet are affected by or interact with operations. The Michigan Department of Environmental

Quality (DEQ) serves as an example of the broad range of external stakeholders. The Department's mission statement simply states that:

> The Michigan Department of Environmental Quality promotes wise management
> of Michigan's air, land, and water resources to support a sustainable environment,
> healthy communities, and vibrant economy. (About MDEQ, n.d.)

Some key words to pick up on in that statement are environment, communities
and economy. These give us clues as to the scope of their impact. Environment
is somewhat easy to understand in the context of an environmental protection
organization. Although it may seem strange or abstract, perhaps an external
stakeholder for the DEQ is the environment itself. This would include rivers,
lakes (particularly important to Michigan), forests and wildlife. Although
this may depend on an individual assessment of the import of these natural
resources, they are certainly within the DEQ's sphere of influence. A new
policy issued by the dredging projects program, for example, would have
a direct and immediate impact on certain waterways, fisheries and coastal
zones.

Communities may be among the more traditional lines of thinking when it
comes to stakeholders. This would certainly include people, groups, schools,
parks, community centers and so on. Another example of stakeholder impact
would be the air quality toxic screening levels program. If the agency relaxes
the guidelines regarding certain airborne toxin levels, who will this impact?
Simply everyone that breathes the air! And their mission statement says they
want to promote "healthy communities."

This brings us to the final group in the DEQ's mission statement. A vibrant
economy may be a tough idea to define or agree upon, but certainly we would
have to consider the business community to be a major component of that
economy. Newly reduced air toxin standards would impact the business community. They would probably impact employee health in the long run. People
may not want to go outside as often, potentially reducing patronage to retail
organizations. But what if they are a manufacturing operation? This reduction
in air standards might have a positive impact on their bottom line. If the DEQ
loosened regulations on air pollution, this might reduce the costs of operating
an automobile manufacturing plant, which would be a positive move for
a certain group of stakeholders.

An environmental agency also provides an introduction to an important
idea in organizational analysis, "competing stakeholders." Competing stakeholders exist when the demands of multiple stakeholders for a given project or
organization are in opposition with each other. In our environmental regulation
example it is likely that many in the manufacturing community may prefer
and vocalize their preference toward the reduction in air quality regulations

while at the same time other groups, perhaps community organizations or environmental interests, may demand that these regulations either remain in place or be made more extensive. The first step is to recognize the existence of competing demands by stakeholders and identify those specific conflicts within an agency's scope of influence.

As another example of competing demands, one that is likely salient to many larger cities in the US, is a long running debate between policing methods in the US. On one side are those who support relatively more aggressive tactics commonly associated with "broken windows" policing. This type of policing often involves aggressively pursuing lower level offenses such as littering, vandalism and jay-walking, and is thought to establish a clear message regarding the type of behaviors that are and are not permitted. Put rather more eloquently by Xu, Fielder and Flaming in their 2005 work on the subject:

> Widespread physical and social disorders break down the existing system of informal social controls and the mechanisms regulating social interaction. As a result, crime proliferates and fear overwhelms. Therefore, it is imperative for police agencies to include disorder control as a strategic measure to prevent crime and community decline. (Xu, Fielder and Flaming, 2005)

Another method is often referred to broadly as "community policing." This theory contends that many aspects of policing are not direct enforcement of laws, but rather serve a more community-oriented or social cohesion function. This approach to policing is often highlighted by more direct involvement by the community in crime reduction, more accountability for police departments and improves service to the community (community satisfaction often being a measure of this) (Goldstein, 1987).

There is clear potential for the existence of competing stakeholders in both the allocation of public resources and the processes by which a public organization enforces laws and reduces crime. Vocal parties exist on both sides. An important first step is to recognize and identify the existence of competing demands early in this performance system process so that these issues can be addressed effectively later on. Public organizations have to be conscious of a broad range of stakeholders, both human and non-human (as illustrated by examples such as the environment and financial assets). Again, the first step in ensuring an organization is responsive to its stakeholders is to identify them.

It is also important to recognize the difference between direct and indirect stakeholders. The International Financial Corporation (member of the World Bank Group) offers a preliminary method of identifying direct and indirect stakeholders through a process called "impact zoning." The language used by the World Bank is geared toward land policy but can easily be broadened to fit most public agency types. Here are the four steps to take when conducting impact zoning (World Bank, n.d.):

1. Sketch a map of the key design components of the project, both on and off site, that may give rise to local environmental or social impacts (e.g., the project site; ancillary infrastructure such as roads, power lines and canals; of air, water and land pollution).
2. Identify the broad impact zones for each of these components (e.g., the area of land take, air and water pollution receptors, etc.).
3. After identifying and mapping broad stakeholder groups, overlay those groups over the impact zones.
4. Through consultation with relevant stakeholder representatives, verify which groups are potentially affected by which impacts. This exercise may be performed more efficiently by using aerial photographs.

It is necessary to first define the realm of influence a particular initiative has, and then identify all the potential stakeholders within that realm. For example, what would the realm of influence be for a municipal Department of Public Works (DPW)? Certainly the area within the city boundaries is relevant. And if the DPW maintains the water system, perhaps the municipal water source, typically outside the city limits, is also within its realm of influence. If the DPW deposits municipal waste and recycling at facilities outside the city's boundaries, these facilities may also be within the realm of influence. It is important to be thorough when determining who may be affected by the totality of operations in order to avoid creating "orphan stakeholders."

To prevent the creation of orphan stakeholders, it is important to understand the difference between direct and indirect stakeholders. Timothy Rowley (1997) defines indirect stakeholders as influential agents of a focal organization that do not have direct relationships with that organization, but still work in the focal firm's interests For our purposes, we can take this to mean any person, group or organization that either works for or is impacted by the focal organization, but is not explicitly cited as a target or primary entity by the focal organization.

To illustrate this point, consider the controversial issue of prisons. A prison is meant to house those who pose a tangible threat to society or have been deemed worthy of punishment through incarceration for some adverse activity. Ideally, prisons keep our communities safe and offer a means by which our criminal justice system can carry out its mandates. Having said that, the direct or primary stakeholders that come to mind are the community which is being protected from crime and the individuals and agencies within the criminal justice system that use prisons as an enforcement mechanism. However, how are we to consider the prisoners? Are those being incarcerated a stakeholder group? Certainly they are being impacted by the operations of the prison, but we often tend to forget the prisoners in our strategic analysis. The purpose of using this example to illustrate indirect stakeholders is because prisoners are often a perfect case of orphan or forgotten stakeholders. We often hear news stories about seemingly endless stints in solitary confinement or rampant violence and abuse of prisoners in facilities across the country. This could be partly caused by prisoners having little to no consideration in our policies. They are not typically considered stakeholders in terms of our evaluation, and thus we lose sight of the impact our actions have on them. If the purpose of incarceration is purely punitive, then not considering prisoners as indirect stakeholders is warranted. But, if our criminal justice system is at least partially concerned with rehabilitation, prisoners absolutely deserve consideration as an impacted group.

Going back to the analysis tools provided by the International Finance Corporation, we are presented with a list of questions to ask when evaluating initiatives and realms of influence (World Bank, n.d.). They are:

- Who will be adversely affected by potential environmental and social impacts in the project's area of influence?
- Who are the most vulnerable among the potentially impacted, and are special engagement efforts necessary?
- At which stage of project development will stakeholders be affected (e.g., procurement, construction, operations, decommissioning)?
- What are the various interests of project stakeholders and what influence might this have on the project?
- Which stakeholders might help to enhance the project design or reduce project costs?
- Which stakeholders can best assist with the early scoping of issues and impacts?
- Who strongly supports or opposes the changes that the project will bring, and why?
- Whose opposition could be detrimental to the success of the project?
- Who is it critical to engage with first, and why?
- What is the optimal sequence of engagement?

Overall, in engaging stakeholders it is critical to recognize their potential influence on the project.

- Position and organization.
- Internal/external: internal stakeholders work within the organization that is promoting or implementing the policy; all other stakeholders are external.
- Knowledge of policy: the level of accurate knowledge the stakeholder has regarding the policy under analysis, and how each stakeholder defines

the policy in question. This is important for identifying stakeholders who oppose the policy due to misunderstandings or lack of information.

- Policy position: whether the stakeholder supports, opposes, or is neutral about the policy, which is key to establishing whether or not he or she will block the policy implementation.
- Determination of Interest: the stakeholder's vested interest in the policy, or the advantages and disadvantages that implementation of the policy may bring to the stakeholder or his or her organization. This helps policymakers and managers better understand his or her position and address his or her concerns.
- Alliances: organizations that collaborate to support or oppose the policy. Alliances can make a weak stakeholder stronger, or provide a way to influence several stakeholders by dealing with one key stakeholder.
- Resources: the quantity of resources – human, financial, technological, political.
- Power resources: the leverage available to the stakeholder, and the ability to mobilize allies. This is an important characteristic that is summarized by a power index and will determine the level of force with which the stakeholder might support or oppose the policy.
- Power: the ability of the stakeholder to affect the implementation of the policy.
- Leadership: the willingness to initiate, convoke or lead an action for or against the reform policy. Establishing whether or not the stakeholder has a leadership role will help policymakers and managers target those stakeholders who will be more likely to take active steps to support or oppose the policy (and convince others to do so) (Schmeer, 1999).

When formulating policies and procedures, this knowledge will help public administrators prioritize the ways in which they engage stakeholders throughout the process. Some individuals or groups may require more convincing or coaching than others. Some may require significant training and some may be inherently opposed to an initiative and pose a fundamental risk to its success. With this information in hand, they can allocate their time and effort more efficiently, less time will be wasted on groups who are already bought into the system and more time will be spent where it is most productive.

PERFORMANCE LEADERSHIP

Making performance happen across these three dimensions – measurement, accountability and trust – is not simple. Public sector performance improvement projects or strategies are not the simple "common sense" solutions typically posed by politicians, the public and the business community: "cut the fat" or "cutback management," "economize" or "privatize," "work harder" or "work smarter," or be more "businesslike." If only such prescriptions were all that public organizations needed, then government's efficiency and efficacy would not be perceived as issues. Simple, naive prescriptions, however, are not very useful. They are contrary to the complex, problem-solving processes government (or virtually any organization) requires in order to address society's most difficult-to-solve problems such as crime, pollution, global warming, health care or education. Rather, the provision and improvement of services, as they actually operate in governments, in their nonprofit partners, or in the most profitable private sector firms is a sophisticated and complex process. It begins with leadership.

In the 1970s, when the term was "productivity" rather than "performance," the U.S. Office of Management and Budget launched a venture into measuring and managing performance in the public sector. The Joint Financial Management Improvement Program was formed and from this initiative came one of the first guides to using data to improve performance. Although technology and procedures have changed since 1977, one critical component is still, and always will be, the importance of top-level leadership. In their report (United States, 1977), they write:

> The first step in developing a productivity program should be the establishment of a central focal point for leadership of the productivity effort. The central point should be near the top of the organization and the director of the productivity unit should have direct access to the head of the organization ... There is no substitute for active leadership from the head of the agency.

The State of Massachusetts "MassResults" program, headed by the Office of Commonwealth Performance, Accountability, and Transparency (CPAT), was a performance initiative to expand the usage of performance management in the state. The first critical success factor was "Leadership": "These types of endeavors succeed or not for many reasons; however, it is evident that all successful systems have in common a strong desire for performance from top leadership" (Meekins and Harmon, 2014).

"Leadership" can be a vague statement: "The answer to any problem is leadership." Well, what does that mean? First, we have to identify what the role of leadership is when it comes to organizational performance. Bob Behn of Harvard University, in his 2014 book *The PerformanceStat Potential: A Leadership Strategy for Producing Results*, presents us with a list of the essential tasks to be performance by leaders, these are:

1.   Articulate the organization's purpose
2.   Identify the organization's performance deficits
3.   Set the targets for eliminating or mitigating those deficits

4.   Identify the initial strategies for achieving these targets
5.   Decide what data need to be collected and analyzed
6.   Initiate the problem-solving discussions to determine what strategies are
     working, what ones are not, and why
7.   Help the organization learn
8.   Motivate people to contribute significantly to the effort
9.   Follow up to ensure that commitments have been fulfilled (Behn, 2014)

This is obviously a pretty tall order. Along with all the other duties of a leader, they must actively guide the organization through its performance journey. An executive must act as a catalyst for change; they must break the cycle of the status quo and disseminate a vision of performance through the rest of the organization. A performance-oriented leader is willing to allow data to change his or her mind. They are able to move beyond pure intuition and lead with a mixture of charisma and objectivism.

For example, "CitiStat," a government-wide data tracking and measurement system in Baltimore, did not just emerge organically. It took the pressure from a newly elected mayor, Martin O'Malley, to implement this reform. In 1999, when O'Malley was elected, the city had experienced chronic budget short-falls, outrageous absenteeism including an average of one in seven employees failing to report to work each day in the Department of Public Works, and ballooning overtime costs (Perez and Rushing, 2007). It is easy to identify the major barriers to this new system of transparency. The status quo was comfortable and it paid well. However, in the face of tremendous pushback from line managers and employees, O'Malley implemented CitiStat and the first project he decided to tackle was overtime and absenteeism. In the very first year of CitiStat, the city saved over $13 million. Overtime fell by 40 percent in the first three years of the initiative and several departments observed a 50 percent decline in absenteeism (City of Baltimore, n.d.).

At the US Environmental Protection Agency (EPA) in 1991, Rich Guimond stepped into his new role as the head of the Superfund program in the EPA's Office of Solid Waste and Emergency Response (OSWER) under tumultuous circumstances. The Superfund program began in 1980 and was formed in order to clean up various sites that had been contaminated with hazardous materials and other pollutants. In 1991, there were roughly one thousand Superfund sites and the EPA had completed cleanup of only six, out of a thousand, in ten years of operation. The criticism over the program's lack of efficiency was intense and growing. Guimond quickly discovered that the only measure of productivity for the program was "deletion" or full completion of a project, not the most illustrative of an operational indicator. The new director quickly organized a meeting of all top managers and asked a simple question, "why is this program not working and what can we do to fix it?" It was noted that the program had been following an 11-step process for completing a site cleanup, and although many of these steps were arguably important, this process could take years. It was concluded that the organization could reasonably reduce this list from 11 to two, and a new site manager would review the cleanup process for completion. This streamlining led to the program achieving an 80 site completion per year average over the next ten years, up from an average of less than one per year in the previous ten years. It took the focus and commitment of a new top manager to spark the conversation that eventually led to a complete performance overhaul (Innovative leadership, 2011).

Writing for the IBM Center for The Business of Government, Shelley Metzenbaum of the University of Massachusetts Boston wrote a performance management recommendation guide for the 2009 presidential transition series. In it, she indicates that performance starts with the president. She makes seven recommendations for the president:

1. Clearly Identify Presidential Priority Targets.
2. Appoint a Chief Performance Officer and create a White House performance unit.
3. Run goal-focused, data-driven meetings.
4. Increase analysis.
5. Engage performance management expertise for the cabinet.
6. Identify and manage cross-agency targets and measures.
7. Adjust accountability expectations (Metzenbaum, 2009).

These recommendations illustrate the need for a leader as a catalyst. The creation of a new unit and the appointment of a new cabinet officer require the power of a chief executive. The actions described above set the tone for the new administration.

Not all leaders are up to the task of revitalizing their organization's efforts for performance improvement. Even if their agency is ready for change, a chief executive might not have the characteristics needed to succeed and bring about real change. In his 2012 book, *Key Performance Indicators for Government and Non Profit Agencies*, David Parmenter discusses barriers to performance leadership; he lists several CEO characteristics that organizations should avoid:

1. CEOs who lack the knowledge to have the requisite expertise to run the organization.
2. CEOs who are completely unaware of the management thinking or literature because their pursuit for learning ceased soon after graduation.
3. CEOs who are motivated to retain the existing measurement system because they benefit from the flaws with large year-end bonuses.

4. CEOs who are addicted to action and quick fixes rather than a well-thought-out, slow but effective implementation of change.
5. CEOs who are happy to run the business on intuition rather than on facts.
6. CEOs who have become immune to waste, who have worked with so many dysfunctional systems that they consider them part of the surroundings.
7. CEOs who have very narrow understanding of the work of leading leadership and management writers, such as Peter Drucker, Jim Collins, Peters and Waterman, Gary Hamel and Jack Welch (Parmenter, 2012).

Obviously all of these traits do not perfectly align with public organizations, "large year-end bonuses" most notably. However, they do paint the picture of a leader who is both risk averse and attached to the old way of things. Performance program leaders must be willing to disrupt, to follow up.

DISRUPTING: GENERALLY ACCEPTED PERFORMANCE PRINCIPLES (GAPP)

Public agencies, in particular large bureaucracies have a tendency to settle into a regimen that evolved over the years and may not be performance oriented. Individuals, both managers and employees, are likely invested in this system. They have a strong interest in maintaining things as they are because they are comfortable. This is what we refer to as performance atrophy, the creative juices have stopped flowing after years of inactivity.

Disrupting the old way of doing things means making it explicitly clear that change is happening. Although performance leaders will face opponents to the new way of doing things, by setting expectations upfront, the transition will be easier. They must be willing to make some enemies, as successes become apparent, and this may even mean finding new line managers that are willing to carry the banner of performance.

A "disruptive" synthesis of necessary performance actions, drawn primarily from practice across the US and the 50-plus countries that are members of The Commonwealth Organization, poses necessary and critical questions for the establishment and continued operation of government performance management systems. Sixteen "Generally Accepted Performance Principles" (referred to by the Secretary General of the Commonwealth earlier in this chapter) codify criteria for improving the quality of a government performance management system (GPMS) (Holzer and Trivedi, 2023). Those 16 principles are summarized in the questions that follow:

1. What is the performance measurement system used by your government's GPMS?

- Is it based on a foundational agreement on the meaning of performance? Does it employ instruments such as a Performance Agreement, Performance Contracts, Results-Framework Document, etc.?
- Does the GPMS cover all aspects of organizational performance? Financial, physical, quantitative, qualitative, static and dynamic?
- Does it focus on "managerial" performance as well as "agency" performance?

2. Does your government's GPMS use an appropriate performance measurement methodology?
   - Is there a connection between (line of sight) vision, mission, objectives, actions and success indicators (Key Performance Indicators – KPIs)?
   - Are the objectives, actions and KPIs in the GPMS prioritized (i.e., weighted)?
   - Is there an explicit, beginning agreement on what constitutes excellent, good, average, and poor level of performance?
   - In your government's GPMS, are you able to calculate a composite score (a weighted index) for managerial performance?

3. Does the GPMS cover the Whole of Government?
4. Does the accountability for results and delivery trickle from the top down?
5. Is the accountability assigned explicitly and unambiguously to specific individuals in the government?
6. Does your government's GPMS have an appropriate incentive system?
   - Are the incentives explicit or implicit?
   - Are the incentives financial or non-financial?
   - Are the incentives related to departmental, team and individual performance?
7. Is the GPMS effectively integrated with the HR systems in the government?
8. Is the GPMS integrated with the budget system?
9. How transparent is your GPMS?
   - Are the commitments and promises made (objectives, actions, and targets) displayed transparently at the inception of the performance program?
   - Are the results achieved at the end of the year actually displayed at the end of the year?
10. Are there appropriate institutional arrangements for managing GPMS?
    - Is there provision for independent (pre and post) expert scrutiny of targets and KPIs?
    - Is the body managing GPMS placed at the highest possible level in the government?
11. Does your government employ an effective communications strategy in all phases of implementing GPMS?
12. Does the GPMS have a strong and unambiguous legal foundation?

13. Is there widespread recognition that performance measures enhance decision making, performance assessment, accountability, service delivery, public participation, civic discourse, problem solving, etc.?
14. Is there complete agreement that citizen-driven performance measurement will add value and utility to internal managerial efforts?
15. Are there efforts to inform performance management via systematic searches for best practice innovations?
16. Is there anticipation of the commitments and efforts necessary for continuous improvement of the performance measurement and improvement process?

PERFORMANCE LEADERSHIP

A performance leader may initially be the only one who will follow up on performance. A common situation is at a meeting where someone asks a question and someone else says they will "look into it," but how many times did that question get answered at the next meeting? How many times did that topic fall into the ever-growing storage closet for all the forgotten meeting topics? If the leader makes clear to everyone that he or she will bring the question up at the next meeting, then they have begun to re-shape the way things work in the organization. They begin to set an example for everyone else. And importantly, they will show that this performance effort is not just a fad. They are in it for the long run and this is the new way of things.

Leadership involves learning, and it is important for leaders to learn, personally, across three facets of performance: data, best practices and findings from the literature. All too often those capacities are delegated, reducing a performance leader to a relatively superficial convenor of team meetings. Knowledge is, of course, power, and a leader's mastery of performance will enhance their power to bring about tangible and positive interventions.

LEARNING TO LOVE DATA

Eventually, performance leaders will want to hire dedicated data analysts to build up the overall organizational capacity. However, as Parmenter (2012) discussed in his list of CEO deficiencies, it is critical to have at least a basic understanding of the use of data to make decisions. Specifically, performance leaders will want to learn what data systems their organization uses and what data their organization collects. If they can speak intelligently on the topic of performance data, other managers might very well follow. A leader needs to be both charismatic and competent in the tasks of the organization. If they do not know how to look at data, they will not be able to make objective decisions based on it.

Performance measurement may seem daunting. But experience across many performance projects indicates that building a data-driven performance program is surprisingly simple and direct, and does not necessarily require complex programming. Five understandings regarding measurement are key:

First, measures are widely available:

- Key Performance Indicators, or KPIs, are based on recognized best practices.
- New or modified measures are regularly published based on practice.
- Users have full discretion on which measures to use or disregard.
- Customized KPIs can be developed for any service area.

Second, data entry is simpler than might be assumed:

- Automatic transfers of data, while preferable, may require complex coding, to begin, however, data can be transferred manually from existing reports.
- Valuable data, often collected but "buried" in reports and databases, can be "mined."
- Data-driven performance programs do not necessarily need dedicated staffing.
- Exporting data to standard spreadsheets provides easy accessibility for developing graphics and sharing data.

Third, performance data can be benchmarked against:

- Targets
- Past performance
- Similar jurisdictions
- Best practices/Award-winning cities

and then:

- Analyzed by a consortium of peer users sharing data and discussing ideas for improvement.

Fourth, dashboards can be constructed, updated and data shared by:

- Reporting the data in graphic formats that are salient to all stakeholders using standard graph and chart formats.
- Updating data regularly.
- Exporting reports quickly to pdf, jpg or PowerPoint formats.

Fifth, discussion of data trends and comparisons can stimulate problem-solving discussions:

- Reluctance to publish data can be overcome by *requiring* sharing of data with all stakeholders: managers, front-line employees, top elected and appointed officials, citizens, the media, etc.
- Authorized users should be able to view a dashboard on the multiple plat-forms: computer, tablet or smartphone.

LEARNING FROM SUCCESSES OF OTHER PERFORMANCE PROGRAMS

Pride may prevent people from seeking advice or guidance from dissimilar organizations. However, best practices are everywhere. Sometimes new ideas can bring a sense of excitement and energy into an agency that has operated in the same manner for years. As one of the founding fathers of American administrative study, Woodrow Wilson wrote in his seminal 1887 article "The study of administration,"

> If I see a murderous fellow sharpening a knife cleverly, I can borrow his way of sharpening the knife without borrowing his probable intention to commit murder with it; and so, if I see a monarchist dyed in the wool managing a public bureau well, I can learn his business methods without changing one of my republican spots. He may serve his king; I will continue to serve the people; but I should like to serve my sovereign as well as he serves his. (Wilson, 1887)

Overall then, by breaking away from the old way of doing things, leaders show that change is ahead. Disruption is the first step in a cultural evolution. Committing to the reforms is key to granting permanence to the new culture; it prevents performance improvement from being a fleeting idea. Continuous and relentless follow-up sets the tone for performance expectations. Looking outside for inspiration can lead to the adoption of practices and philosophies that may have never before been considered by the agency. For example, the National Center for Public Performance convenes an annual international conference at which performance innovations are showcased and discussed (Box 3.1):

BOX 3.1   FIVE TAKEAWAYS FROM THE NATIONAL CENTER FOR PUBLIC PERFORMANCE 2019

Public Performance Conference

The National Center for Public Performance held its annual Public Performance Conference at Suffolk's Institute for Public Service in late September 2019. Featuring speakers and attendees from around the world, the event explored cases and presented solutions from local, state, and federal government agencies, as well as nonprofits and private consulting firms. Here are five takeaways from the two-day conference:

1. Sweat the small stuff

Keynote speaker Brian Elms is a founding member of Peak Academy, which has helped the city of Denver save millions of dollars by empowering city employees to make changes and improvements and solve problems on their own. The key to the innovations? "They're simple, small, and cheap," he said.

Elms explained that communities need to look for incremental change and constantly ask themselves: Can we fill another pothole today? Can we return someone's lost dog so that we don't have to feed and house it? Can we serve another child today? Can we take another person off the street? "If we each were doing one better thing every single day, we would see an improvement in our overall work," Elms said in his keynote address.

2. Being strategic is, well, a good strategy

Mark Abrahams, who earned his MBA at Suffolk in 1982, was an early implementor of Performance Management in the United States, working with the cities of Indianapolis, Milwaukee, Boston, and many others. His commonsense revelation for these and other communities he's worked with? Set overall goals, preferably in the form of a strategic plan. "What does the community want? What are the major outcomes they want to achieve? And can they articulate that so that departments can develop program plans and goals?" he asked. Abrahams' overall theme was that alignment from the top down leads to better outcomes.

3. Make your data indispensable

In a talk entitled "Don't Throw the Baby Out with the Bathwater," return presenters Anne McIntyre-Lahner and Ron Schack spoke about the challenges that agencies face when a new government or administration comes in and wants to put their stamp on everything. It can cause a lot of disruption to programs and methods that agencies use. Good, smart thinking about data can be arbitrarily jettisoned.

One solution to sustaining programs in the face of administrative policy changes is to broaden and diversify the list of stakeholders. "Building external constituencies for the data you're producing within an organization is one of the key ways to sustain the production of data," said Shack. "Because if external stakeholders consistently press for those data, it's hard for someone within the organization to just say, 'Oh, don't produce that.'"

4. Imagine a far out solution
That was just one of the many department projects and priorities on MeghanMarie Fowler-Finn's list. She's the performance manager for the District Department of Transportation (DDOT) in Washington, DC. With a yearly capital budget of more than $650 million, DDOT oversees everything from parking and bike lanes to school crossing guards and forestry – and possibly a gondola at some point. The dynamic is especially complex because the District of Columbia is a hybrid city-state, which means different reporting structures and budgeting challenges than in the 50 states.

Fowler-Finn and her team have been working to help people across DDOT use data to make informed decisions, a concept she called "data power." The goal is to ensure that everyone has a shared truth. Once that's achieved, then everyone can drive measurable change and action.

5. Efficient silos don't make an organization efficient
Contributing an international perspective was Prajapati Trivedi, who leads the Economic, Youth, and Sustainable Directorate of the Commonwealth Secretariat in London. In his presentation, he pointed out that while performance management can certainly help different parts of an organization run more efficiently, it doesn't necessarily mean that all those parts work together well. What's needed to make silos collaborate better are "team targets," or, in other words, making all the silos responsible for a single outcome.

One example he related: When the Indian government wanted to produce more electricity, it had to get five different government agencies to work together. The solution Prajapati's team suggested? Give the agencies team targets and incentivize them to work together. All the agencies were told they would share in the success – or failure – of the project. After that, the government was completely hands off: the agencies had to handle it themselves. "We defined the goal for the constituencies and told them, 'You're big boys. You figure out how to deliver. It's your problem,'" Trivedi said. The result? The agencies met their targets and produced the extra 20,000 megawatts.

Source: Holzer (2019).

LEARNING FROM PERFORMANCE FINDINGS

Smart public and nonprofit managers recognize that performance management and improvement is a multifaceted endeavor that offers opportunities for creative and meaningful problem solving. *The Public Productivity and Performance Handbook*, Third edition (Holzer and Ballard, 2023), for example, advances a set of findings that characterize effective government performance programs. These lessons are inconsistently and inadequately taught in public administration programs and are almost never apparent in practice under political and budgetary pressures. They can be summarized as a series of evidence-based conclusions and recommendations (Box 3.2 is an overview). Each of the Findings in Box 3.2 is synthesized from the handbook.

> **BOX 3.2   FINDINGS FROM *THE PUBLIC PRODUCTIVITY AND PERFORMANCE HANDBOOK*, THIRD EDITION (HOLZER AND BALLARD, 2022)**
>
> * Finding #1: Building a culture of performance management should not be taken for granted.
> * Finding #2: Performance reforms may be short-lived if support is not "cultivated" across highly complex and politically governed institutions.
> * Finding #3: Stakeholders need help in understanding the data.
> * Finding #4: Performance programs must be aware of what works, what does not, and what to avoid.
> * Finding #5: Managing for high performance requires tools and support.
> * Finding #6: Measurement and analysis guide performance programs.
> * Finding #7: Performance budgets and audits are necessary complements to a performance program.
> * Finding #8: Intelligent human resource management contributes to peak performance.
> * Find #9: Performance programs can help renew public servants.
> * Finding #10: Organizational innovations offer extensive possibilities for creative, measurable progress.
> * Finding #11: Accessing and adapting best practices is a valuable, but often overlooked, resource.

Finding #1: Building a Culture of Performance Management Should Not Be Taken for Granted

Performance management is undoubtedly worthwhile but often difficult to adopt, and perhaps even more difficult to implement over time on a sustained basis. Challenges to initial efforts to manage for performance can grow and multiply over time, presenting significant barriers to the continuation of such reforms. Research suggests that organizations need to develop both technical and cultural capacities to implement performance management and use performance information for informed, data-based decision making. Research also suggests requisite technical expertise to collect and analyze relevant data, organizational knowledge of basic performance management concepts, and the "buy-in" of individuals at all organizational levels. All must exist for performance reforms to sustain themselves over time. However, how do you convince employees, who may be resource- and time-constrained in their efforts to perform their primary duties, to take on the additional roles and responsibilities associated with performance management? How do you develop a culture of performance management that pervades an institution and can outlast leadership transitions? How do you develop incentive and reward structures within public organizations to promote data-driven decision making?

Finding #2: Performance Reforms May Be Short-lived if Support Is Not "Cultivated" Across Highly Complex and Politically Governed Institutions

Ever since Richard Nixon, almost every US president has established a management reform agenda. In the early 1970s President Richard Nixon established the National Commission on Productivity and Quality of Work Life, which became a National Center and was then replaced by programs in the Office of Personnel Management under President Jimmy Carter in the late 1970s. In the early 1990s, President Bill Clinton's Administration shifted the government's approach as Vice-President Al Gore led the National Performance Review. From this review came the first large-scale legislative initiative at the federal level, the Government Performance and Results Act, generally known as GPRA. In the early 2000s, President George W. Bush followed with the Program Assessment Rating Tool, or PART, and President Barack Obama replaced that with the GPRA Modernization Act.

Each such presidential initiative was an attempt by Congress and the executive to change the federal bureaucracies' work, which was often emulated at the state and local levels, with the goal of improving productivity and performance. However, each of these initiatives was fraught with challenges. GPRA had significant difficulty developing clear objectives for programs that could then be tracked by numerical measures. PART resulted in merely symbolic use of performance information to satisfy mandated processes and did not actually result in performance improvement, per se. Political ideology and turnover also present challenges to such reforms. And performance management may not be politically attractive or salient to the public.

Finding #3: Stakeholders Need Help in Understanding the Data

Effective adoption of performance management initiatives is not only about using or not using performance information; the presentation of indicators also matters. In fact, the presentation of information can drive how it is interpreted by the readers. This is one reason why the link between better performance does not always result in higher levels of trust in government. There are substantial differences in the way people interpret performance information depending on how it is framed. The positive phrasing of performance reports can lead to a positive interpretation, and by the same token a negative phrasing of performance information can cause individuals to have a critical response.

The development, publication and dissemination of service-specific data may pleasantly surprise the public, the media and elected officials, A foundational element of a performance improvement program is the publication of key performance indicators for a government's core functions. Public performance improvement programs can provide extensive compendia of defined and vetted KPIs in all core service areas, based on recognized best practices, with regular updates. Those indicators typically utilize data "buried" in reports and databases. The data, presented in robust graph and chart formats, can be used to benchmark performance against targets, against past performance and against the performance of similar organizations. The data can drive problem-solving discussions among a broad range of stakeholders, including citizens and their surrogates.

Finding #4: Performance Programs Must Be Aware of What Works, What Does Not, and What to Avoid

It is important to be aware of the kinds of strategies that work, those that do or do not have a successful track record, and obstacles or impediments that must be avoided. Public organizations may face many challenges when implementing organizational performance: data collection processes and systems may need to be put in place, personnel may need to be trained, software may need to be purchased. Certainly, these are potential challenges organizations may encounter on their organizational performance management journeys. However, the biggest challenge an organization may face, and the challenge that must be overcome in order to be successful, is total support of top management for the effort. Organizational performance management must become part of the culture of an organization, part of its very fabric. And an organization must be able to show top management, after a reasonable period, that it is better off for having implemented organizational performance management than it would have been otherwise. Results matter. Organizational performance management cannot be just a data collection exercise.

Finding #5: Managing for High Performance Requires Tools and Support

Sound public management and competent public managers are critical to the efficient delivery of necessary, impactful public services. Public administrators require the appropriate tools and support systems to carry out their missions. Those resources include employing:

- Strategic planning to better align the organization to an anticipated future environment.
- Performance management to assess organizational performance in the implementation of strategies.
- Both new and old technologies.
- Analytic tools.
- Public-private partnerships and hybrid organizations.

Finding #6: Measurement and Analysis Guide Performance Programs

Measurement is at the heart of productivity and performance management. What is almost an obsession with measures can be traced from the early twentieth century to today's "stat" programs. Data is necessary, but certainly not sufficient, for as complex an initiative as a performance improvement program.

Managers must strengthen their decision making by using evaluation information, applying it to help them continually improve the effectiveness and efficiency of their services. Managers are continuously making program decisions throughout the year, and need varied information to make those decisions, especially evidence on how effective and efficient their services have been, in answer to the following types of questions: How are we doing? Are we getting the results we want? Are we making progress in improving the lives of our citizens?

When there is agreement on goals – what should be done – then accountability efforts, including performance measurement and evidence-based practice, can contribute to improvement. When that is not the case, when questions are framed within the purview of the political domain, then the same efforts will result in fruitless endeavors that collect considerable data, contributing to the policy discourse but not to improved implementation.

Performance management for performance improvement is the process of defining, monitoring and using objective indicators of the performance of organizations and programs to inform management and decision making on a regular basis. This provides a way for organizations in the public and nonprofit sectors to be accountable to citizens, clients and funders. In addition, performance measures support other management and decision-making processes, such as budgeting, grants and contract management, and program evaluation. The ultimate goal is that this information will be utilized to improve overall program performance. In the public sector, programs of evaluation and their associated goals play a key role in delivering services to constituents, facilitating operations and enhancing quality of life.

Despite substantial growth in data collection and reporting capacity across governments, a much smaller cohort of governments has been shown actually to integrate this information into their planning and evaluation routines. Extensive research into the adoption-use gap highlights an important consideration for modern public administration, suggesting that the mere existence of data does not mean governments will operate more efficiently or provide higher quality services.

Finding #7: Performance Budgets and Audits Are Necessary Complements to a Performance Program

Performance responsibility contributes to fiscal responsibility. And in terms of fiscal responsibility, two performance approaches are particularly important – performance budgeting and performance auditing.

A line-item budget illustrates where public money is to be spent item by item. However, the idea behind performance budgeting is that how much you spend on department x is tied directly to how well department x is performing. Performance budgeting requires the establishment of performance levels and the collection of information (or data) that relates whether those performance levels have been met. The most common types of performance indicators are outputs and outcomes. Output indicators report units produced or the quantity of services provided by a department, an agency or a program. Outcome indicators reflect how well a government entity is meeting its goals and objectives. These indicators are designed to answer questions that deal with the quality and impacts of government service delivery. The central points of performance budgeting are: (1) the amount of work that is done is measured; (2) the quality (or the results) of that work is measured; and (3) this impacts how much money a department will receive in the future. Departments that overperform may receive more money, while those that underperform may receive less. Critics argue that using performance measurement as a basis for determining budgets is counterintuitive because taking money away from a struggling department is likely to make matters worse. Also, some might argue that measuring performance is inherently problematic; that is, designing performance indicators is subjective, and collecting data can be time-consuming and expensive.

Finding #8: Intelligent Human Resource Management Contributes to Peak Performance

Very little that is meaningful in public service can be delivered by robot. Human interaction is an essential element regardless of policy domain. Whether public health or education, transportation or energy, law enforcement or public transit, the public encounter – where citizen and state meet – is where feelings erupt and where feelings reflect and shape attitudes toward the state. A power differential is always present and colors the exchange. The encounter is wrapped with meaning, and the aftermath of the interaction has a significant impact on citizen engagement and confidence in government. Mindfulness is important regarding the citizen-state encounter.

Find #9: Performance Programs Can Help Renew Public Servants

Performance projects and programs have another, often unrecognized, advantage. They should not be viewed as just highly technical, data-driven efforts that are delegated to a small team of specialists or consultants. They also present opportunities for reenergizing public servants who, as the humanities suggest, may have become jaded by the bureaucratic environment, who go along to get along; but rather than suffering in silence, eager to take on new challenges they could become government's internal consultants. Most public servants would look forward to applying their problem-solving skills, building their competencies, and bringing about meaningful improvement in promised services in the public interest. Public organizations need to make the most of those motivated human resources by giving them more room to innovate, to problem solve, to be creative rather than confining them to the stereotypical bureaucratic mold. "Bureaucrats" are government's creative problem solvers, and it well serves government to give them a much wider range of opportunities to engage in improving systems and services, outputs and outcomes.

Finding #10: Organizational Innovations Offer Extensive Possibilities for Creative, Measurable Progress

The productivity-performance toolbox has evolved over the course of the twentieth century. But demands for more rapid improvements in public services are inducing public managers to consider a wide range of innovations. Such innovations include advanced technologies, public-private partnerships, and wider, deeper sets of competencies.

Positive change is occurring when it comes to performance improvement – especially in the innovative use of advanced tools and technologies as applied to performance measurement. For those who call home the field of public policy and administration, the mantra has been both constant and consistent – is it effective, is it efficient, and in recent years is it equitable? How do we prove it? What measures do we use to justify our policy and procedural outcomes? For certain, the only way to move beyond soundbites and rhetoric is for us to develop better performance measurements that are transparent, duplicative, and for all to see, comprehend – and hopefully – take action.

The functional performance of local government institutions can be significantly improved by enhancing the organizational capability and culture. That involves equipping the organization with the needed intrinsic motivation, expertise, flexibility and cohesion to attain its goals. Finding potentially applicable innovations requires expertise: identifying databases, searching extensively and efficiently, accessing the details of promising cases, and selecting the most applicable possibilities. Those competencies are most readily brought to the table by the appointment of an Innovation Officer, and all large public agencies should be required to create and fill that position; smaller agencies could easily share that type of position. Investing in an Innovation Officer is likely to have a high payoff even for small localities and agencies:

- Identifying innovations with potentially fast and sustained paybacks.
- Scanning for innovations nationally and globally.
- Serving as an internal consultant and model for all employees, especially managers.

Finding #11: Accessing and Adapting Best Practices Is a Valuable, But Often Overlooked, Resource

Public sector organizational innovations, or performance-enhancing models, are available for the taking, but few jurisdictions avail themselves of those resources. Too many public managers assume their work, their services, their populations are a unique mixture. Although thousands of award-winning or

Table 3.1   Search terms for researching for best practices

Primary	Secondary		
Awards	Award-winning		
		C	
Best Practice	Best	o	
Cases	Case Studies	m	
Examples	Excellence, Exemplars	b	Government
Honors		i	Public
Innovations		n	Agencies
		e	Departments
Models	Model Programs	d	Programs
Outstanding			Systems
Performance	Government Performance, Public Performance	w	
Quality	Quality Management	i	
Recognition	Recognized	t	Specific Services
		h	
Top Ranked	Top Rated		

benchmarked projects and programs are readily available on the web, that knowledge base is an underutilized resource with potentially high returns.

Performance management and improvement would profit from the systematic identification and application of best practices that have been singled out as award-winning innovations. Thousands of innovations in the delivery of public services are recognized annually, yet public and nonprofit professionals often overlook these resources.

These are programs which address society's most difficult problems: providing no-cost medical care for the indigent, unclogging court calendars, installing pollution and flood controls, expanding the supply of decent housing, increasing critical services to senior citizens, rehabilitating youthful and older offenders. Such problem-solving efforts are neither unique nor limited. They are easily and freely identifiable on the web using applicable search terms (Table 3.1). And once identified those programs are typically eager to share their models, their "lessons learned," and even their manuals and systems. Those cases are rich resources for decision-makers seeking examples of policies, interventions and programs that potentially can be adapted to improve services and outcomes for the public.

LINKING RESEARCH AND EDUCATION TO PRACTICE AND PERFORMANCE

The "Performance Movement" has built an extensive set of resources for strategic performance improvement across the broad range of promised public services. That body of knowledge offers an avenue for rebuilding public trust by delivering on government's promises. Evaluation and policy analysis classes spend much of their time on economic concepts and data collection techniques, and only discuss performance in the abstract, missing the important link between data and organizational leadership and culture.

One option for remedying this education-application gap is to offer performance concentrations in MPA and MPP programs. A four-course concentration, offered at Suffolk University-Boston in conjunction with the National Center for Public Performance, is built around four pillars (Institute for Public Service, 2022):

Course I. Performance Improvement Strategies

History of performance improvement initiatives: successes and failures. Beginning with, and linking to, the mission statement. Why measure performance? Governance by the numbers. Building capacity for performance: the organization's culture, mission and processes. Leadership for performance. Political authorities and the politics of performance. Adopting, but not implementing, a performance program. Performance stat. Performance measures and reports. Creating a culture of performance management. Employee empowerment. Strategic and performance plans. Performance-informed organizations. Comprehensive performance improvement systems. Institutionalizing performance.

Course II. Performance Measurement Capacities

What types of performance information should be tracked? Basic performance system outline. Identifying and monitoring performance system deficiencies. Reporting for the sake of reporting. Defining and operationalizing objectives. Setting and communicating targets. Creating goals and objectives. Becoming results oriented. Outcome, rather than output, orientations. Key Performance Indicators (KPIs). Reliability and validity. A logic model perspective. Intended vs. unintended incentives.

Course III. Relating Performance to Stakeholders

Data collection, analysis and visualization. Types of surveys, sampling, recognizing errors, crafting questions. Data availability. Data costs. Limits of data. Benchmarking. Open data. Basic statistics: correlation, causation, scatter plots, etc. Visualizing information for: citizens, managers, political officials, interest groups, funders, the media, etc. Citizen participation. Improving trust by citizens/stakeholders. E-government. Utilizing social media.

Course IV. Connecting Measurement to Performance Improvement

Measurement as indicative of opportunities to improve or to share innovations. The role of incentives. Moving to performance-based budgeting and performance-based management. Sharing and consolidating services. Partnership government. Utilizing information resources. Searching for applicable, recognized innovations: web-based searching for best practices and award-winning programs; networking across organizations and borders; accessing professional resources.

A means for empowering practitioners of public performance who have diverse degrees and professional identities, but who are not likely to return to the classroom to earn MPA or MPP degrees, is a non-credit performance certificate. Such public performance management certificates should be offered on all training menus at all levels of government, and might well utilize self-paced, independent study.

An even more powerful path to building capacities for performance would be to legislate legal certifications for "public performance managers," certifications that would require regular continuing education requirements such as those now mandated for attorneys, architects and many other licensed professions. Examples of such?

A few public performance certificates are now offered, often online. The Strategic Performance Management Certificate of the National Center for Public Performance (2022), for example, emphasizes setting objectives, a logic model, reporting and data visualization, stakeholder analysis, behavior barriers, and turning data into action. Hundreds of practitioners have earned that certificate. Some other performance certificates are generic, addressing the needs of industry as well as government, a more technical approach that minimizes the distinctly different political, cultural and behavioral barriers that characterize the public sphere. The public sector needs and deserves performance training specific to its culture and context, and such training needs to be widely available, even legally mandated. The value of the results will far exceed the investments.

The Performance Checklist (Box 3.3) is a comprehensive synthesis of performance course content across formal courses and online certificates.

BOX 3.3   PERFORMANCE CHECKLIST

Plan Strategically

- Secure Top Leadership Involvement and Commitment
- Consult with Key Stakeholders
- Understand Prior and Related Efforts
- Ensure Sufficient Resources to Begin Program
  - Human Resources
  - Budget Processes: Short Term/Long Term
  - Invest in State-of-the-Art Technologies/Software
  - Invest in Learning Resources: Conferences, Courses, Best Practices, etc.
- Develop a Strategic Plan for Performance Measurement and Improvement
- Develop Performance Goals and Sub Goals
- Set Performance Improvement Priorities, Starting with Potential High Impact Areas
- Connect to the Organization's Overall Strategic Plan
- Connect to Strategic Communication Processes
- Ensure Access to Organizational Data
- Develop Individual and Team Performance Incentives

Build Capacities for Measuring and Improving Services

- Form Internal Performance Working Group(s):
  - Employees, Citizens/Users, Management/Executives, Performance Experts
- Form or Link to External Performance Working Groups:
  - Similar Communities, Professional Associations, etc.
- Train Key Staff in Performance Analysis Competencies
- Access Lists of KPIs: Online and Print/Books
- Select KPIs (Quantitative/Qualitative) for Capacities
- Select KPIs for Outputs/Services
- Select KPIs for Outcomes/Impacts
- Access Routinely Collected Data
- Target Data That Has Not Been Routinely Collected

- Conduct Surveys/Interviews of Users, Non-Users, Employees, Managers, etc.
- Build Dashboards/Develop Graphics
- Publish Report Cards: Data + Vignettes

Learn for Performance Improvement

- Continually Access the Relevant Literature/Networks/Data
- Convene Performance Measurement and Improvement Meetings
- Emphasize Learning from Successes and Errors
- Scan Tracked Data and Trends to Identify Areas for Improvement
- Search Networks and the Web for Best Practices and Model Programs
- Contact Best Practice/Model Programs to Discuss Subtleties
- Disseminate Best Practices Models to All Stakeholder Representatives and Members of Performance Working Groups
- Adapt Best Practices to the Local Context
- Implement Decisions to Improve Services and Outcomes
- Coordinate with Personnel Performance Evaluations
- Develop Individual Incentives/Shared Rewards
- Develop Team Incentives/Shared Rewards

Engage Partners to Maintain and Build Momentum

- Build a Successful Track Record of Small Wins
- Celebrate Wins Internally
- Publicize Wins Externally
- Expect Crises and Misunderstandings/Be Prepared to Respond with Facts
- Build Capacity to Meet Increased Demands for Services
- Continually Scan the Political/Managerial/Labor Environment
- Communicate Regularly with Community-based Partners: Nonprofits, the Public, Interest Groups
- Educate the Media
- Build Public-Private Collaborations
- Highlight Track Record of Performance Improvements in the Budget Process
- Constantly Supply Elected Officials with Evidence of Successes
- Argue That the Performance Program is the Organization's Best Investment/Return on Investment (ROI)

TAKEAWAYS

- Public organizations must deliver on government's promises if government is to build trust with its stakeholders.
- Public programs serve a surprisingly broad array of stakeholders, internal and external, direct and indirect, some of which have competing agendas.
- Performance leadership is critical, complex and continuous.
- Performance leaders can disrupt old, unproductive ways by following Generally Accepted Performance Principles (GAPP).
- Performance initiatives must: plan strategically, build capacities for measuring and improving services, learn for performance improvement, and engage partners to maintain and build momentum.
- Performance leaders should be models by learning to: love data, understand the successes of other performance programs, and apply performance findings from published analyses.

SELECTIONS FOR FURTHER READING AND RESEARCH

Validated Evidence That Performance Programs Work

Publications
Public Performance and Management Review (1974–2023). https://www.tandfonline
   .com/toc/mpmr20/current
Publishes peer-reviewed research on the performance of public-facing organizations, advancing theories on measurement, management and achievement of promised outputs and outcomes.

Ammons, D. (2019) *Performance Measurement for Managing Local Government: Getting it Right.* Thousand Oaks, CA: Melvin & Leigh Publishers.
An indispensable guide to the design, construction and utilization of public sector performance measures at the local level.

Barrett, K. and Greene, R. (2020) *The Promises and Pitfalls of Performance-informed Management.* New York and London: Rowman and Littlefield.
A very practical, readable and in-depth guide to measuring, analyzing and improving performance in public organizations, with a particular emphasis on avoiding potential problems.

Behn, R.D. (2014) *The Performance Potential: A Leadership Strategy for Producing Results.* Washington, DC: Brookings Institution Press/Ash Center.
Superior explanation of CompStat as a pathbreaking approach to data-driven analysis of public performance programs, initially in the field of policing, and then extending to other public services.

Berman, E. and Hijal-Moghrabi, I. (2022) *Performance and Innovation in the Public Sector: Managing for Results*. New York and London: Routledge.
Applying scholarship to practice, this well-researched and well-written volume offers a broad set of tools with which to take advantage of the most current public management paradigms.

Bryson, J.M. (2018) *Strategic Planning for Public and Nonprofit Organizations*. Fifth edition. Hoboken, NJ: Wiley.
The "bible" of strategic planning, this text is a comprehensive set of building blocks toward accomplishment of any public agency's mission.

Holzer, M. and Ballard, A. (eds) (2022) *The Public Productivity and Performance Handbook*. Third edition. New York and London: Routledge.
Building from the assumption that a productive society is dependent upon high-performing government, this third edition of *The Public Performance and Productivity Handbook* explores all of the core elements of improvement from the perspectives of many of the leading experts in the field.

Julnes, P. and Holzer, M. (2008) *Performance Measurement: Building Theory, Supporting Practice*. Armonk, NY: M.E. Sharpe.
Includes methods and techniques for developing effective performance measurement systems, building performance-based management systems and sustaining performance-based budgeting.

Hatry, H. (2007) *Performance Measurement: Getting Results*. Second edition. Washington, DC: Urban Institute Press.
Addresses every component of the performance measurement process from, arguably, the most engaged expert in the field; addresses the program's mission, objectives, customers, trackable outcomes, finding the best indicators for each outcome, the sources of data and how to collect them.

Lu, E.Y. and Willoughby, K. (2018) *Public Performance Budgeting: Principles and Practice*. New York and London: Routledge.
One of the only books that looks at performance measurement and evaluation in relationship to all phases of the budgeting process.

Scott, R. and Boyd, R. (2022) *Targeting Commitment: Interagency Performance in New Zealand*. Washington, DC:Brookings Institution Press/Ash Center.
This book explores how and why the New Zealand government made progress on the Better Public Services program, sustaining the commitment of public servants and unleashing the creativity of public entrepreneurs.

Networks
U.S. Federal Government Performance Improvement Council. Source: Performance.Gov
How US Federal Government managers set strategic objectives and achieve cross-agency priority goals.

The Center for Accountability and Performance (CAP) of the American Society for Public Administration. Source: https://aspacap.com
Presents awards for systemic change as evidenced by measurement of results and documented impacts.

Results for America. Source: https://results4america.org/
Outlines standards of excellence for data management, analytics and evidence-based decision making at the municipal level.

National Center for Public Performance. Suffolk University-Boston. Source: https://www.publicperformance.org
Conducts conferences and pursues research in performance measurement and improvement. Offers related online certificates in strategic performance management and other areas.

REFERENCES

About MDEQ (n.d.) GreeningDetroit.com. Retrieved August 4, 2022, from https://www.greeningdetroit.com/member/michigan-department-of-environmental-quality/
ASPACAP (2020, July 22) The Center for Accountability and Performance (CAP) presents its annual awards in a first-ever virtual awards ceremony on Thursday, July 23, at 2pm EDT (detailed award information below). American Society for Public Administration Center for Accountability and Performance. https://aspacap.com/2020/07/22/the-center-for-accountability-and-performance-cap-presents-its-annual-awards-in-a-first-ever-virtual-awards-ceremony-on-thursday-july-23-at-2pm-edt-detailed-award-information-below/
Barrett, K. and Greene, R. (2020) *The Promises and Pitfalls of Performance-informed Management*. New York and London: Rowman and Littlefield.
Behn, R.D. (2014) *The PerformanceStat Potential: A Leadership Strategy for Producing Results*. Cambridge, MA: Brookings Institution Press/Ash Center.
CHOGM Opening Ceremony – a "free association of self-governing nations." (2022, June 24). The Round Table [video content]. https://www.commonwealthroundtable.co.uk/commonwealth/chogm-opening-ceremony-a-free-association-of-self-governing-nations/ and transcribed September 21, 2022.
City of Baltimore (n.d.) Baltimore CitiStat. https://data.baltimorecity.gov/
David Ammons receives 2020 Joseph Wholey Distinguished Scholarship Award (2020). UNC School of Government. https://www.sog.unc.edu/about/news/david-ammons-receives-2020-joseph-wholey-distinguished-scholarship-award
Freeman, R.E. (1984) *Strategic Management: A Stakeholder Approach*. Cambridge: Cambridge University Press.
Goldstein, H. (1987, January) Toward community-oriented policing: Potential, basic requirements, and threshold questions. *Crime & Delinquency*, 33(1), 6–30.
Holzer, M. (2019) *Five Takeaways from the National Center for Public Performance 2019 Public Performance Conference*. Newark, NJ: National Center for Public Performance.
Holzer, M. and Ballard, A. (eds) (2022) *The Public Productivity and Performance Handbook*. Third edition. New York and London: Routledge.

Holzer, M. and Trivedi, P. (2023) *Generally Accepted Performance Principles.* London: The Commonwealth.

Holzer, M., Callahan, K., Carrizales, T., Hammond, K., Harris, G., Kang et al. (2011) Citizen-driven Government Performance. Newark, NJ: National Center for Public Performance. http://web.pdx.edu/~stipakb/download/PA555/Citizen-DrivenGovtP erformance.pdf

Innovative leadership in government: One example of how it can make a difference (2011) FedSmith. Retrieved July 29, 2015, from http://www.fedsmith.com/2011/03/ 04/innovative-leadership-government-one-example-how/

Institute for Public Service. Suffolk University. Master of Public Administration Concentration in Public Performance (2022).

Maxwell School (n.d.) Master of public administration program mission statement: Lead the way to a better future for all. Syracuse University Maxwell School of Citizenship & Public Affairs. Retrieved August 1, 2022, from https://www.maxwell .syr.edu/academics/public-administration-international-affairs-department/public -administration-all-programs/master-of-public-administration/mission-statement

Meekins, R. and Harmon, M. (2014) Performance management toolkit: Improving results in the public sector. Retrieved July 29, 2015, from http://www.mass.gov/ informedma/docs/final-toolkit7-21-2014.pdf

Metzenbaum, S.H. (2009) Performance management recommendations for the new administration. Edward J. Collins Center for Public Management Publications, Paper 11. https://scholarworks.umb.edu/cpm_pubs/11/

Parmenter, D. (2012) *Key Performance Indicators for Government and Non Profit Agencies: Implementing Winning KPIs*. Hoboken, NJ: John Wiley & Sons.

Perez, T. and Rushing, R. (2007) The CitiStat model: How data-driven government can increase efficiency and effectiveness. Center for American Progress, 5.

Performance framework (n.d.) Performance.gov. https://trumpadministration.archives .performance.gov/about/framework_about.html

Public Performance Management and Review (n.d.) Taylor & Francis Online. https:// www.tandfonline.com/journals/mpmr20

Rowley, T.J. (1997) Moving beyond dyadic ties: A network theory of stakeholder influences. *Academy of Management Review*, 22(4), 887–910

Scheminske, E.R. (2015, September) Colorado Performance Management Program overview. Panel session presentation at the 2015 Public Performance Measurement and Reporting Network Conference, Newark, NJ.

Schmeer, K. (1999) Section 2: Stakeholder analysis guidelines. In *Policy Toolkit for Strengthening Health Sector Reform*, 1–33. Bethesda, MD: Abt Associates Inc.

Sharma, R. (2008, October) The 6 principles of stakeholder engagement. *Supply Chain Management Review*, 12(7), 1–8.

State of Colorado's Office of State Planning and Budgeting (Scheminske, 2015).

Strategic Performance Management Certificate: Now enrolling – summer 2022. (2022) National Center for Public Performance. Retrieved August 4, 2022, from https:// www.publicperformance.org/strategic-performance-managment

United States Joint Financial Management Improvement Program (1977) Implementing a productivity program: Points to consider. Washington, DC: Joint Financial Management Improvement Program.

Wilson, W. (1887) The study of administration. *Political Science Quarterly*, 2(2), 197–222.

Working with stakeholders (n.d.) https://gcn.civilservice.gov.uk/guidance/how-to -guides/working-with-stakeholders/

World Bank (n.d.) Stakeholder Identification and Analysis. International Finance Corporation. Retrieved August 5, 2022, from https://www.ifc.org/wps/wcm/connect/ e7705f54-6cd2-44b8-87fb-609a87a3f4a9/PartOne_StakeholderIdentification.pdf ?MOD=AJPERES&CVID=jqetJIm

Xu, Y., Fiedler, M.L. and Flaming, K.H. (2005) Discovering the impact of community policing: The broken windows thesis, collective efficacy, and citizens' judgment. *Journal of Research in Crime and Delinquency*, 42(2), 147–86.

4. Bureaucratic resistance as ethical persistence

BATTLE BUREAUCRACY

Bureaucracy is, by its nature, averse to dissent. Orders flow from the top, and top-level officials do not want to be embarrassed or contradicted. Yet the reflexive suppression of dissent may result in tragic and expensive errors that could have been avoided if concerned bureaucrats had been empowered to share their apprehensions.

Public servants want to act ethically. While many bureaucrats take issue with their organizations' leadership and policies, few are moved to dissent in the public interest. Those are the few who must not be suppressed, but rather should be heard. Those are the "bureaucratic canaries" in the organizational mine alerting the leadership, the media and the public to the largely unintended consequences of policies that were once well intentioned, but are now harming individuals, groups or the general population. Bureaucrats may also be alerting the public, and its media and legislative surrogates, to unethical, illegal, destructive behaviors of their superiors.

Resisters are keepers of the organizational conscience, of the oaths of office, or the ethical standards that drew them to public service. They help public bureaucracies protect the public from cancer-causing air and water, from toxic chemicals, from corrupt behaviors. They do so by quietly building the evidence, forcing independent reviews, meeting with like-minded staff, earnestly talking to their superiors about incompetence and malfeasance. If necessary, they take the risk of blowing the whistle, leaking information as to criminality and publicly confronting higher officials. They are a resource to be appreciated, not punished.

Public administration degrees and in-service training need to equip public servants with an unorthodox "toolkit" of professional options for countering organizational missteps, blunders, oversights and miscalculations. Bureaucrats need to feel supported across a range of options that will protect the public while enabling their agencies to deliver services as promised. And they need to know what those options are.

Many recruits enter government with high ideals and good intentions to serve the public. They want to "make a difference," to "give back," to "dedicate their lives to improving the lives of others." They often put their own lives on the line as police, military, emergency workers, firefighters and public health workers, and even as teachers, nurses and doctors. For many, their sense of satisfaction, of contribution, of engagement is more important than the size of their paycheck.

Well-intentioned public servants, however, too often accede to a culture of: "go along to get along," "blow the whistle and blow your job," and "whatever the boss says to do is OK." That reluctance often leaves their agencies in the dark regarding mismanagement, corruption and malfeasance.

The costs of willful organizational ignorance as a function of their protecting their jobs are, all too often, dramatic disasters. Bridges collapse from poor design or lack of maintenance. Pandemics spin out of control. Wars are launched to serve someone's ego. Life-saving drugs are locked in warehouses. Students are left to drift without competent instruction.

Countering that indifference, however, requires giving bureaucrats much more involvement and discretion, or "buy in," than they are customarily afforded. As participants in their agency's problem-solving processes, as service providers whose suggestions are welcomed in the improvement processes, as long-time observers whose accumulated knowledge can be invaluable, they can be an organization's "prepaid" consultants, acting within and beyond their formal job descriptions. Participation and recognition help them consider the agency's missions as their own, appreciate the need to open communications with clients, and encourage meaningful working relationships with those clients. That chemistry results in stronger service delivery.

In order to maximize the contributions and performance of all of their public servants, public organizations must recognize that:

- Important decisions require input from everyone (not just top managers) who can be important to those decisions. If some mid-level bureaucrat or front-line employee knows why plans "A" and "B" will fail, but "C" will succeed, giving them a forum may well avoid major mistakes.
- Listening to prepaid employees is much more economical than hiring well-paid consultants to improve processes that lead to performance.
- Because having access to information is necessary for making better decisions, that data must be available to bureaucrats who are involved in performance-improvement problem solving. Effective data sharing must be regular, honest and clear.

How to engage employees in meaningful problem solving is complicated. In pursuit of involvement, public administration has experimented with Total

Quality Management, Quality Circles, and countless other participatory innovations. The top-down classical organizational culture, however, is still prevalent. The typical, traditional work environment – as the humanities repeatedly remind us – is still suffocating. MPA/MPP curricula and parallel in-service training need to equip bureaucrats who resist such an environment with a toolkit of professional strategies that will enhance their abilities to "do the right thing," all the while avoiding seeing their agencies take egregious, harmful and counterproductive actions, albeit unintended.

A central tenet of this book, and of bureaucratic resistance specifically, is to do the right thing. Although organizational professionals often raise critical issues, they are typically ignored or punished to the detriment of the public good. Resisting illegal orders and criminal behaviors is a high calling to support the interests of the citizenry, of the constituents the organization is meant to serve. That expectation applies to all levels of government, from the small three-person office at the local level to the seemingly endless national enterprise at the federal level.

Options for quiet resistance to questionable instructions or commands are surprisingly abundant, but often neglected as points of discussion in the public administration classroom. Students are largely left to figure these strategies out on their own or with their colleagues on the job, resulting at best in an incomplete and inconsistent menu of options. If quiet professionalism is not effective, then bureaucrats who are committed to correcting policies should consider a set of public-facing options, with the associated career risks that they entail. The full range of strategies for "Battling Bureaucracy" are summarized in Box 4.1, Strategies for Bureaucratic Resistance, and each is discussed in detail below.

BOX 4.1   STRATEGIES FOR BUREAUCRATIC RESISTANCE

- Identify as a Professional
- Build a Case
- Persist
- Use Visuals to Make the Case
- Enliven the Data with Stories and Images
- Exercise Discretion
- Play by the Book
- Recommend Remedial Action
- Emphasize Costs and Savings
- Recruit Allies

- Alert Decision-makers
- Communicate Alerts through Special Channels
- Transfer Offices (or Not)
- Resign in Protest
- Refuse Illegal Orders
- Leak Information
- Petition
- Blow the Whistle
- Lawyer Up

IDENTIFY AS A PROFESSIONAL

Professionalism as resistance hinges on the assumption that to violate one's profession would be to violate the responsibilities of one's position. Management may sometimes, however, ask the doctor, nurse, lawyer, accountant and the countless other professionals within the bureaucracy to conduct themselves against their professional expertise for political reasons. The professional, by focusing on doing their job properly, resists.

It is important to keep in mind that this strategy can be psychologically troubling. There is the natural inclination that being professional and upholding one's professional responsibilities is an intrinsic good. When this intrinsic good is questioned by superiors for political gain, or for personal gain, and is coupled with implicit threats of retaliation, what is the professional supposed to do? Forsake the profession and keep the job? Or forsake the job and uphold the profession? Even if no one else is aware of an individual's loyalty to professional guidelines, there is an inner voice commending such integrity. It is important to realize that professional actions have implications for policy and politics, and maintaining a professional orientation may be countering whatever inappropriate or illegal actions some superiors may have in mind.

When resisting, the bureaucrat should make every attempt at projecting a professional, civil demeanor. Being labeled an obstruction is not a helpful identity for enacting meaningful change. The resistor must manage issues with professionalism and respect. The resistor's language should be respectfully critical. Coming off as a jaded and vengeful subordinate bent on "getting even" with one's supervisor should not be the primary motivating factor of one's resistance.

This strategy can provide a "double benefit" in which the resistor comes off as sincere and respectful, while the organization can become increasingly the "bad guy" for retaliating against such a concerned individual. Upon first knowledge of an abuse, the bureaucrat should not storm up to the supervisor's office yelling and screaming. This will quickly make the situation worse.

Professional licenses and accreditation can be used as a defense against inappropriate requests. This type of resistance can be particularly effective if the organization's capacity is contingent on specific licenses or accreditations. An example would be a higher education institution that needs accreditation for its enrollments, advertising, and its very existence. One can also leverage the specific licenses one might have as a doctor, lawyer or other specialized profession. For instance, if a superior demands that the bureaucrat act on a certain order that goes against the oaths and regulations of that profession, the bureaucrat has firm grounds to argue against that action. The statement might go as follows: "As an accountant, if I follow that order I would be in violation of my CPA credentials and my license could be revoked."

But it is important to keep in mind that supervisors may not be satisfied with this answer and demand that the bureaucrat implement the policy anyway; this strategy can buy time, eventually forcing reformulation of the policy within professional guidelines.

Jacqueline Verrett began work in 1958 at the Food and Drug Administration (FDA) and a decade later would inadvertently become a whistleblower, calling attention to the artificial sweeteners that contained cyclamates. Her media interview about reports concerning cyclamates would lead to the ban of cyclamates in 1969 (Nader, Petkas and Blackwell, 1972, p. 90). Upon first discovery of cyclamates dangers, she reported her findings internally to her FDA supervisors for years – to little avail. But when the media happened to ask her about the cyclamates, she felt no hesitation in telling them what the FDA should have already known. Also, her office was featured in FDA films, and other news releases (Nader, Petkas and Blackwell, 1972, p. 92). Thus, she had the impression that the media was not a "scary" actor to interact with. There was also supporting research circulating around the scientific community about the subject, and she was not divulging anything "new" in her interview.

After the interview she was hardly retaliated against, and was actually promoted a few years later. Perhaps this is the "perfect storm" situation for those who wish to dissent, but what made her dissent successful was her excellent professional credentials and societal pressure on FDA concerning cyclamates. She knew the research, she was confident to talk about it, and her credentials spoke for themselves.

BUILD A CASE

A solid case built on experiences, notes, documents and records is critical to any resistance or whistleblowing effort. Being proactive with the support of data collection, with appropriate data distribution, and by speaking "truth to power" can build a reputation of thoroughness. Even though digital information is common, a resistor still ought to consider the strategy of maintaining records and finding print evidence that proves an abuse. Hard documents facilitate the possibility of using other tactics, such as leaking information, lawsuits or cultivating outside support.

The bureaucracy, whether on the state, local or federal level, is characteristically a mountain of paperwork. Unprepossessing paper files in manilla folders, or digital records in computer files, are perhaps the best spots to hide injustices. Even though digital information is common, a resistor still ought to consider the strategy of finding hard paper evidence that proves an abuse. Hard documents may still facilitate the possibility of using other strategies, such as leaking information, lawsuits or cultivating outside support.

Building a case does have some cautions that the resistor should keep in mind. Documents can be labeled classified, and inappropriately holding onto classified information can lead to legal action and possible termination. Another caution to keep in mind is one's position in the organization in relation to the records obtained. For example, if the resistor has sole access to information that happens to be leaked, the organization might easily trace who leaked those items. Thus, the bureaucrat must keep in mind who has access to what information, who sees what information, and the general importance of the information that is being maintained.

"Copy the Controversy" is a related physical action in which the resistor, after finding hard documents of abuse, copies the documents for future use. This can be controversial by itself since the resistor is "stealing" information that might then be leaked to outside agents. The resistor simply has to take incriminating documents and proceed to the copy machine.

Ron Ridenhour was a Vietnam War veteran who investigated the My Lai massacre by the American military a month after it was orchestrated. His research would horrify him and provoke a 1,500-word letter to President Richard Nixon, Secretary of Defense Melvin R. Laird, and members of Congress concerning the massacre and its cover-up (Cushman, 1998). That missive led to convictions, and resignations, after it went public via the *New York Times*. While Ridenhour was dissatisfied with the outcome, his letter helped build a culture of resistance to the Vietnam War by publicizing the horrors that occurred.

Vladimir Bukovsky, an author, activist and dissenter, lived in the Soviet Union and helped orchestrate a 1965 protest in Pushkin Square, earning him 12 years in prison at hard labor (Berlinski, 2016). He earned notoriety for smuggling resistance records outside of the USSR. Those records detailed the abuses in the USSR's psikhushkas – political psychiatric hospitals (Berlinski, 2016). The maintenance and smuggling of the documents would shine light on the horrors of the Soviet Union, and would later be published in the Soviet Archives.

First-hand primary sources are important for resistance efforts. Especially if the information is "self-evident" to the point that little actual explaining needs to be done by the resistor, and the documents prove the point of the abuse in their own words. Such evidence becomes almost irrefutable by the organization perpetuating the abuse and the resistance is greatly strengthened. Bukovsky's name is often mentioned with other famous dissidents such as Alexander Solzhenitsyn, Andrei Sakharov and Yuri Orlov (Berlinski, 2016).

The famous case of Daniel Ellsberg and the "Pentagon Papers" is the prime example of "copying the controversy." Daniel Ellsberg was a military strategist who studied at Harvard and strongly disagreed with the escalation of the Vietnam War. While working at the RAND Corporation, he was tasked with a top-secret report analyzing US decision making from 1945 to 1968. After being inspired by a colleague, Randy Kehler, and readings from Thoreau, Gandhi and Martin Luther King, he decided to copy the 7,000-page document and leak it to the *New York Times*. "The Pentagon Papers," in Ellsberg's words, were "evidence of a quarter century of aggression, broken treaties, deceptions, stolen elections, lies and murder" (Staff, Biography, 2014). This leak would lead to the New York Times Co. v The United States case ruling that the press could print the Pentagon Papers without risk of government censure (Staff, Biography, 2014). Ellsberg would galvanize the anti-war movement, engendering a climate of skepticism that would carry over to the Watergate Scandal, and to other dissenters wishing to voice their particular concerns.

PERSIST

One of the most important strategies when resisting implementation of a policy is persistence. It can be easy to become discouraged when a resistance effort is not slowing the pace of unjust policies, or when the resistor suffers retaliation. Persistence is a necessary strategy given how long some resistance efforts might take, especially concerning legal matters. Generally, then, persistence is a characteristic in almost all resistance efforts, and a necessary characteristic at that. Bureaucratic resistance is not for the weary or the faint of heart.

Persistence can, however, be wished away. Resistors may see an injustice and think that if they merely raised the concern in a meeting that everything would be resolved. But an individual can become jaded, disillusioned and depressed by how much persistence is necessary when pursuing a resistance effort. Even if they know it may take some time to fully remedy the problem, a resistance effort that takes years to fully materialize might dissuade most from taking on the project to begin with.

Many cases of resistance show the importance of persistence, and persistence can truly make a moment into a movement – a movement that can change an industry, an administration or the culture of an organization. Persistence can support the resistor who purposefully slows an organization's productivity, such as the whistleblower testifying before Congress. Persistence is almost always necessary; without it, little is likely to be accomplished.

Simply inquiring further into an abuse can help move the resistance effort forward. This strategy is particularly helpful early in the resistance effort while the resistor still has access to individuals, records and personnel. This strategy aims not only to clarify the abuse, but to gain more information on the different aspects of the abuse. This cuts both way as the alleged abuse may only seem like a critical situation from the outside. Once the potential resistor learns more about the phenomenon, however, it may lose its luster and tensions may subside. Conversely, inquiring more thoroughly about an abuse may provide important data for future resistance efforts.

A hopeful aspect of this strategy is how the potential resistor may exercise pressure through such inquiry. The potential resistor can ask probing and uncomfortable questions into questionable practices. A superior, once being questioned, may realize the abuse is ethically questionable, and instead of backing off may create excuses or be dismissive. The information may be surprisingly forthcoming depending on the culture and individuals involved. The organization may have been perpetuating the abuse for years and it is simply how "it has always been done." If this is the case, gaining information may be easier, but stopping the abuse may actually be more difficult given the organization's acceptance of the practice. It is important to get questions and answers recorded, in writing or on a recording, for future use if needed.

While inquiring further can be a simple discussion, it can also be a forceful legal action. Freedom of Information Act (FOIA) requests are formal ways of inquiring further into an abuse. While the process can be time consuming, new information can strengthen and renew resistance efforts.

Michael Quint was a senior construction inspector on the Los Angeles Metro Rail (Miethe, 1999, p 154). As a civil engineer and expert with over 30 years of experience, he reported deficiencies in safety regarding subway construction (Miethe, 1999, pp. 154–5). The safety concerns largely dealt with adequate expenditures, where not enough reinforcing concrete, steel and supports were in place to completely defend against leakage and accidents (Miethe, 1999, pp. 155–6). Quint was persistenct in reporting the problems. He met with the FBI, he met with the district attorney, he wrote letters to various officials and politicians, he gave presentations on the deficiencies, and he even wrote to President Clinton on the subject (Miethe, 1999, pp. 157–8). Quint did suffer retaliation for his dissent in the form of termination, but his efforts led to a change in policy in which modifications were implemented with no further taxpayer expense (Miethe, 1999, p. 163). Quint moved necessary change forward, and without his persistence the safety of Los Angeles transit riders would have been jeopardized (Stein, 1992).

Norm Buske was also quite persistent. He was an oceanographer who fought the Navy almost single-handedly to strengthen environmental standards at Puget Sound Naval Shipyard. Buske would investigate water pollution levels surrounding military bases (Miethe, 1999, p. 187). After discovering the Puget Sound facility failed two of his tests concerning radiation, he began to voice dissent concerning environmental regulations and compliance (Miethe, 1999, p. 188). Buske would swim out to the test locations dozens of times to check compliance, even being arrested by Navy police for trespassing (Miethe, 1999, p. 189). The judge would dismiss each case, but shortly after the dismissal Commander V.T. Williams issued an order that "in some cases, [it is author-ized] to shoot to kill swimmers approaching" (Miethe, 1999, p. 190). The risks were drastically increased. Buske's persistence, and the support of the Government Accountability Project (GAP), led to a successful court defense to allow him to continue studying the waters of Puget Sound (Miethe, 1999, pp. 191–2). Persistence was key and continued even after his exoneration at trial. Accountability, while not a sexy concept, requires the individual or over-sight organization to be vigilant and persistent in the pursuit of justice.

USE VISUALS TO MAKE THE CASE

For a resistance effort to be successful, the resistor should put the data into usable, visible and powerful formats. Simplifying the data is a meaningful step in changing organizations or behaviors. Displaying the data in meaningful charts, graphs and correlations can help the resistance efforts in many ways. Data must be communicated to relevant stakeholders in appropriate meetings, a task more amendable to graphics than to spreadsheets. If the intent is to present (or leak) data to the public, to the extent that it is easily visualized by the general population it can elicit responses more quickly. Graphic presenta-tions help management better understand the concerns, abuses and potential remedies. Graphic data makes one's own resistance efforts easier as spread-sheets and tables are not necessarily salient to the public, the media, much of the workforce and elected officials.

Years of education, experience and technical expertise can foster a propen-sity for jargon as an entirely different language between specialists. This may seem easy, but many specialists and even the press have difficulty utilizing this strategy effectively. It is important that the expert plainly presents the data that affects people in an easy-to-understand format. This strategy can be difficult for specialists who for years have studied the necessary material, and take considerable pride in their knowledge and expertise. That can block the "dumbing down" of the data for average consumption. But simplifying the data is a meaningful step in changing organizations or behaviors.

John W. Gofman and Arthur R. Tampli both worked for Lawrence Radiation Laboratory, in Livermore, California, which was funded by the Atomic Energy Commission (AEC). They researched the standards that the AEC would attempt to implement and voiced concerns, in 1969, that the standards, if met, would create thousands more cases of cancer per year. Thus, they argued, the standards were too lax and needed to be strengthened. Their scientific conclusions were accurate, and even AEC officials agreed, but publication was blocked (Nader, Petkas and Blackwell, 1972, p. 62).

Gorman and Tampli made the information public as a hypothetical causal relationship supported by evidence. They delivered speeches at universities, submitted reports and testified in front of Congress. They also published a provocative book, *"Population Control" through Nuclear Pollution* (Nader, Petkas and Blackwell, 1972, p. 64). Most importantly, throughout this episode they would use "value ladened language" that "cut through the bureaucratic jargon" (Nader, Petkas and Blackwell, 1972, p. 73). They faced retaliation, but overall their efforts were a success. The Federal Radiation Council was abolished and the responsibilities were moved to the Environmental Protection Agency (EPA) (Nader, Petkas and Blackwell, 1972, p. 69). The AEC would propose stricter standards in 1972 (Maugh, 2007).

John Paul Vann, a highly decorated and skilled pilot and commander during the Korean and Vietnam Wars, used statistical methods to show the exaggeration of the numbers of enemy combatants killed in Vietnam. A supporter of the Vietnam War initially, he became disillusioned upon finding that the South Vietnamese forces had little will or experience to fight the Viet Cong, and that civilian casualties were being counted as combatant casualties. Going through internal channels to reform the situation, he was sent back to America at the urging of higher-ups in the field. While back in the US, he presented his report, coupled with interviews and field reports, to Pentagon officials (Kross, 2007). This would earn him allies from generals to fellow resistors. These allies, however, would prove not to be enough, and Vann would retire from the Army in 1963.

He would go back to Vietnam in 1965 with Environmental Protection Administration (USAID). With his previous experience and knowledge of opposition forces, he helped direct and ultimately save allied forces during the Tet Offensive in 1968. Although his reports alone may not have necessarily changed policy in the region, the validation of his reports in the form of the surprise Tet Offensive would force policy change by later administrations (Kross, 2007).

Sam Adams was a CIA intelligence analyst during the Vietnam War. He discovered that twice the number of Vietnamese forces existed than what the official figures were stating (Staff, The Whistleblower Directory) After discovering this data, and the subsequent cover-up by the CIA and Department of Defense, Adams leaked these figures to the *New York Times* (Staff, The Whistleblower Directory) This action, partially emboldened by Daniel Ellsberg, helped advance the resistance dialogue concerning Vietnam. His action also helped prevent an escalation of the war by President Johnson who "would have given General Westmoreland the 206,000 men" he needed to combat the Vietnamese (Staff, The Whistleblower Directory).

ENLIVEN THE DATA WITH STORIES AND IMAGES

The data is much more effective if there is a story behind it. Data can work in calling attention to a problem, but a story can multiply its impact. Eyes can glaze over when talking about data, even easily readable data, whereas cases highlight the importance of the story behind the resistance. Each data point should be complemented by an anecdote: cancer rates with vignettes of individual cancer patients; recidivism rates with sketches of individuals in the correctional system; murder rates with the tragedies of individual victims. Then statistics can tell the larger story.

The prudent bureaucrat, when resisting orders, must understand how imagery can be used to his or her advantage. Images can evoke emotional responses and add multiplying effects to a resistor's efforts. Nobody wants to be known as "inefficient," "unjust," "wrong" or "racist." These words evoke negative connotations that are inseparable from the terms themselves.

It is important then for the bureaucrat to use images to their advantage. If slowing work down to block policy is spun by the perpetrators of injustice as inefficient and bureaucratic (in the pejorative sense) then the resistance effort may already be lost. Thus, the bureaucrat should hold up and monopolize the images of justice, aiming to show that the policy change will better society.

A prime example of effective use of images is the Thalidomide case in the 1960s. Barbara Moulton was a doctor at the FDA during the 1950s who studied the effects of various drugs seeking to come to market. Subsequent to studying the effects of "miracle" antibiotic Sigmamycin, and the unacceptable dangers of its use, Moulton argued within the agency to limit the drug (Johnson, 2003, p. 81). This would lead to retaliation, in the forms of a forced transfer. After the transfer, she testified before the Kefauver Committee, officially blowing the whistle on the FDA. She would relate vivid details of a "cozy relationship" between the FDA and pharmaceutical companies, and how the FDA "insisted on everyone ... being wined and dined" (Johnson, 2003, p. 80). That symbolism was critical as the FDA and government agencies are mandated not to be "cozy" with the organizations they are charged with regulating in the public interest. Shining a light on this phenomenon, and labeling it so, was a fundamental step for bringing about change. Barbara Moulton's efforts yielded change in the organization most dramatically with the forced resignation of Henry Welch, who was the chief of the Antibiotic Division of the FDA at the time (Johnson, 2003, p. 80). After exposing corruption and being retaliated against, she resigned in 1960 (Geng, 1973).

Moulton's efforts, however, set the groundwork for her successor, Frances Kelsey, to land the decisive blow. After Moulton's departure, Frances Kelsey succeeded Moulton. Her first project was a review of Thalidomide. While studying the drug and its deplorable birth defects, she withstood countless pressures inside the FDA, and from the drug companies themselves. She would be harassed by phone calls several times a day from William S. Merrill Company concerning clearance of the drug (Johnson, 2003, p. 84). The situation would get so bad that Kelsey would simply stop answering her phone during the day (Johnson, 2003, p. 85). She would withstand this pressure for two years until the tragic European phocomelia epidemic occurred. Thalidomide was convincingly linked to birth defects, and Kelsey, with her allies, brought to light gruesome images to finally stop the distribution of the harmful drug (Geng, 1973).

Frank Snepp was a survivor of the Vietnam War in which he was a spy for the CIA. After the fall of Saigon, he became disillusioned with how the CIA, and the US generally, handled the war and leaving many of the US contacts in the country to die at the hands of the North Vietnamese. More should have been done, and he had to tell the story. In 1977 he published *Decent Interval*, relating stories of botched evacuations and other tragic incidents in Vietnam (Rabinowitz, 2013). Critics would hail the book as "the single finest record of that shameful episode" and that it was "on par with the leaking of the Pentagon Papers" (Rabinowitz, 2013). But the book was thoroughly challenged by the CIA. The CIA would sue Snepp and the case would go all the way to the Supreme Court, where he lost. Snepp was devastated by the ruling, but firmly believed that information is "an instrument of change" and that the story must be told (Rabinowitz, 2013). His resistance helped define the anti-war literature and make the public more aware of government actions.

EXERCISE DISCRETION

The bureaucrat almost always has discretion. Reality is complex, and rules may shape how individuals respond, but there is always "wiggle-room." Students may receive special attention from teachers. Police may or may not initiate actions after pulling a car over. Foreign service officers may arbitrarily disapprove applications. But such bureaucrats, wishing to resist unacceptable orders, can attempt to exercise discretion. When considering discretion, the bureaucrat should ask the following questions to him or herself: Can I "recruit" colleagues to resist and widen the discretion resistance? Am I willing to maneuver around the rules to prevent bad policy and abuses?

A related possibility is for the resistor to return substandard or inflated services or products. This can be embarrassing to the organization and may make the press. This strategy can be especially potent when the product is deficient, cheaply made or costly. Depending on the position and expertise of the bureaucrat, denying or delaying payments for services and products can halt much of the production process. This is particularly effective concerning procurements, grants and other functions related to physical products or physical services. Examples abound: the procurement officer that works for the Department of Defense notices cost overruns and demands an explanation; the diplomat overseas who sees a foreign government demanding more from USAID without specification for what or where that money will be going; the accountant at the local police department who sees cost overruns on police equipment. Given the cost constraints of government, the natural demands for efficiency, and the willingness of individuals to abuse the system, holding onto funds until the abuse is corrected can be a powerful mechanism.

This strategy assumes that the bureaucrat is in some position to exercise this power, with enough authority and expertise to give weight to such an obstructing action. It is worth keeping in mind that if a potential resistor wishes to use this strategy it could very well conflict with senior executives' demands for such policies to be enacted.

General Tony Zinni was an expert and specialist concerning the Middle East. As commander-in-chief of the United States Central Command from 1997 to 2000, and then appointed a special envoy to the Middle East afterwards, he knew the region and the costs of action (Leung, 2004). He would be terminated from his position by President Bush over his opposition to the war in Iraq, and after the invasion Zinni would state publicly that the planning for the war was a "dereliction of duty, or even corruption" (Leung, 2004). In his opposition, he used his discretional leeway to advocate for overwhelming force in Iraq, the "General Shinseki's view," and not Donald Rumsfeld's concept of small force, high technology (Leung, 2004). Zinni also called the war the "wrong war, at the wrong time, with the wrong strategy" and overall opposed the operation on a conceptual level (Leung, 2004).

PLAY BY THE BOOK

"Sticking to the Rules" is when the resistor follows each rule to the letter without the usual cutting of corners that may occur for reasons of efficiency. Perhaps ironically, "By the Book" is resistance by doing one's job "correctly." The point is that "the book," with its strict and hardly read rules, can be used to slow processes and halt unjust policy. "By the Book" can also be powerful in meetings in which the resistor can point specifically to where a rule conflicts with the supervisor's policy initiatives. Of course, this can create tensions, but it is difficult to argue against. Rules are rules! Of course, this strategy is contingent on the resistor having a thorough knowledge of the manuals, rules, regulations and policies of his or her organization.

With the complexities of federalism, bureaucratic policies and laws, a bureaucrat can often find obscure aspects of policy that can slow or otherwise halt just about any initiative. "Out Ruling the Rulers" is when the bureaucrat, when opposing a policy, finds obscure nuances in relevant regulations that can stall or otherwise stop the policy in its tracks. All bureaucracies have obscure nuances to their codes and conduct that almost any bureaucrat can utilize.

Julia Davis worked as a Customs and Border Protection Officer in San Ysidro Port of Entry (Staff, National Whistleblower Center (2017b). After the discovery of 23 "improperly processed entries" and little urgency on the part of Department of Homeland Security, she followed protocol and alerted the FBI's Joint Terrorism Task Force (JTTF) (Staff, National Whistleblower Center, 2017b). Twenty-three SIC (Special Interest Country) individuals entering the country in the span of a day is uncommon, given that on average 5–15 enter in a given month ("Whistleblowers A-D," n.d.). She was told to cover up the episode until a later date, but instead followed protocol and informed the appropriate departments. Davis received severe retaliation in the form of being labeled a "Domestic Terrorist" and 54 charges were filed against her (Staff, National Whistleblower Center, 2017b). She won the ensuing court hearings, and a documentary was made about the incident, *Top Priority: The Terror Within*.

Paula Broadwell was General David Petraeus's biographer, and had an affair with him in which Petraeus compromised confidential information. The FBI investigated, but slowly. Frederick W. Humphries II was "concerned and frustrated by the high level of direction" in a case where superiors that normally would not be involved were, and overly specific procedures were being followed that normally were not (Tapper, 2015). Humphries testified countless times commenting on the behavior of his colleagues at the FBI, the unnecessary expansion of the investigation, and the seemingly strict use of regulation to halt much of the process (Tapper, 2015). The FBI would be successful in utilizing the "By the Book" strategy, delaying justice until after the elections, but would ultimately bend to Humphries's resistance, causing Petraeus to resign in shame. Just as the resistor can use the rules to stop the presses (or start them), so can the organization in blocking resistors who aim for change. Perhaps counterintuitively, this case shows the use of "By the Book," but by the organization itself.

The Trans-Alaskan Pipeline was proposed in the 1970s in response to the discovery of Alaskan oil. However, The Environmental Quality Act of 1970 mandated that "every federal agency file a public 'environmental impact statement'" if construction projects impact the environment in meaningful ways. Initially, this project was described in reports as nonthreatening to the environment. Anonymous Interior Department dissenters would become outraged and leaked memos to Jack Anderson, a Washington columnist (Nader, Petkas and Blackwell, 1972, p. 172). These leaked documents would make it to Congressman Les Aspin (D – Wisconsin) and be published in the *Congressional Record* (Nader, Petkas and Blackwell, 1972, p.172). This delayed the construction of the pipeline, and brought awareness to the public concerning environmental issues. None of the dissenters were identified.

The employees at the Interior Department knew the rules to use in such a situation. The environmental impact report had to be done, and had to be done right, for a project to move forward. Thus, their insistence and raising of public awareness of this rule delayed the policy effectively.

RECOMMEND REMEDIAL ACTION

While resisting policy is important, providing a meaningful policy alternative or modification to address the problem is even more important. One may think this is a simple "X is bad, the policy recommendation is to not do X," but there are almost always multiple policy options available to decision-makers. The resistor should have a meaningful set of policy alternatives available for discussions with supervisors, superiors and elected officials. A simple "Nuclear energy is unsafe, we must abolish all of our nuclear plants" will not readily win much support or change the industry. However, a resistor taking issue with safety guidelines at a nuclear power plant can attempt to advocate for strong safety regulations in more concrete forms, such as better safety equipment, procedures or additions.

Wayne Handfield was one of the many Colt workers in a 1971 case concerning poor M-16 rifle inspections. Handfield's recommendation was to lessen lead poisoning at the West Hartford, Connecticut plant (Nader, Petkas and Blackwell, 1972, p. 143). Ventilators were not installed in the shooting range where much of the inspections took place. The shooting range contained lead, and many of the Colt workers were contracting lead poisoning as a result. Handfield filed an Occupational Health and Safety Act (OSHA) complaint to the Department of Labor and recommended ventilation be installed. He also went to the press, the *Hartford Courant*, to tell the story of unsafe working conditions (Nader, Petkas and Blackwell, 1972, p. 143). This, plus the OSHA complaint, would bring federal investigators. After the investigation the ventilation was installed.

While a simple case, Handfield's actions illustrate the potency of simple policy recommendations. Shutting down an entire industry is not particularly easy. However, a specific abuse such as lead poisoning, and a specific remedy such as ventilation, is both concrete and localized.

EMPHASIZE COSTS AND SAVINGS

Bureaucrats can convince their organizations or the public as to the financial benefits for the reform. The False Claims Act is an example of this. The government should not be cheated by private contractors, and bringing attention to those issues saves the government money. The more the bureaucrat highlights savings, the more likely their reform will be successful.

Speaking to financial savings essentially aims at creating efficiencies in an organization – to correct the ship when it has gone off course. The bureaucrat then becomes not so much a resistor as a consultant. The bureaucrat consults on what the price of a good or service should be.

To use this strategy the bureaucrat must be well spoken, persuasive, and have strong knowledge of the data. This knowledge of the data must include the "should costs," the "does costs" and the "opportunity costs" of the poor policy. Thus, the bureaucrat must be confident in such a situation.

During the early 1980s the EPA's Seattle regional office was a battleground of resistance. Under John Spencer's leadership between 1981 to 1983, the Seattle office noticed behavior that was odd, unethical, and otherwise against the spirit of the office. Examples included attempting to use taxpayer money to purchase entrance into the Chamber of Commerce, and using public funds for private trips (O'Leary, 2014, p. 48). Bureaucrats in the Seattle office filed an Office of Inspector General (OIG) complaint against Spencer in response. While the OIG report was concluded, and drew a negative image of Spencer, he was not severely reprimanded in any meaningful way (O'Leary, 2014, p. 54). This episode would occur again between 1986 and 1990 under Robie Russell. This time, the Seattle office was willing to fight back in many ways to support the OIG complaint. Staff of the Seattle office would meet secretly to discuss ways to resist and share information about Russell. These secret meetings supported the implementation of other resistance strategies, forcing Russell out of office and creating a culture of dissent (O'Leary, 2014, p. 61).

RECRUIT ALLIES

Allies are important to a resistance effort and should always be in the toolbox of potential resistors. Allies can be found in almost all places, from friends at work, to family, to outside organizations. Allies can artificially create leverage in a situation and act as advocates on behalf of changes in policies and procedures. Allies can provide "cover" from angry superiors. Recruiting allies broadens the range of action for the lone resistor to operate and prevents the individual from being labeled as a "lone zealot." Often, when an abuse is being perpetuated by an organization, the lone resistor finds that they are not the only ones who notice. If a resistor can effectively tap into the concerns of his or her colleagues and see where they stand on the alleged issue, a coalition might form.

This strategy operates on the assumption that the bureaucrat has acquired allies either externally or internally. When superiors know "who they are messing with," then they may be more likely to listen. It is easy for supervisors and superiors to pull the "authority card" and pressure lone bureaucrats to give up the resistance. However, once the bureaucrat has, and alludes to, his or her allies regarding a specific policy or policy implementation, the higher level may well stand aside. Alluding to allies shows the support one already has, and grants legitimacy to the claim that an abuse should be stopped. It is important to keep in mind, as the resisting bureaucrat, simply alluding to one's allies may not remedy the abuse immediately. It may even escalate the situation where superiors allude to their own allies in the hierarchical organizational structure. Thus, mentioning allies can broaden the scope of the conflict. Their mere mention indicates resolve, shows the seriousness of the situation, and signals that the abuse will not be tolerated. A few questions to keep in mind when alluding to allies: Do I allude to all of my allies at once? Or do I highlight the ones most relevant at the time? How might superiors receive the news of a resistance coalition building? Will they increase retaliation? Or will they acquiesce?

However, allies are not a given, and often they can be difficult to find. Recruiting allies requires some sense of salesmanship in which the lone resistor must relate, communicate and convince other actors to join the cause. This can range from a casual coffee during lunch, to after work banter. It may be easier to develop allies when the bureaucrat has been at the organization for some years, or if the bureaucrat has a reputation for professional excellence. This brings up an important note in general – one should cultivate allies and skills outside of and before a resistance effort. A friend of years will more likely join the resistance effort than a stranger with little reason to believe or trust in the resistor.

Many of the people in this chapter have and use allies in their resistance efforts. The cases below indicate specifically how allies have helped resistors achieve meaningful change in an organization. Examples of this can range from formalized groups to the casual after work informal drink (Nader, Petkas and Blackwell, 1972, pp. 173–4). Regardless of the form it takes, finding allies and holding meetings to discuss resistance and strategy can provide many benefits. They can be intangible, such as being able to vent and discuss feelings and emotions about a certain issue. Or they can be tangible in the form of physical support against a supervisor, organization or higher-ups.

The prudent resistor should consider cultivating relationships with outside entities such as professional organizations, advocacy groups and the media. If internal avenues fail to bring about change, allies can lend additional weight and leverage to a resistance effort. This strategy assumes the resistor can "play politics." If the resistor is an introvert scientist who never leaves the office, then utilizing external sources may be difficult. This method of resistance relies on the ability of the resistor to convince, advocate, and ultimately find allies for the cause. Cultivating interest group support is critical to pursuing external means of resistance.

This strategy highlights opportunities for resistors to approach those who are "movers and shakers" within or outside of the organization, and then aims to "woo" them to the resistance effort. The point of this strategy is that bureaucrats with ambitious allies, who are willing to do more than merely sign a letter or say they are a part of the effort, can achieve more impact. In some cases members of the resistance may carry clout as "movers and shakers." Such powerful allies can act as a shield from criticism from those who oppose the resistor, granting more freedom of movement for the resisting bureaucrat.

Jeff Thomas was a quality assurance specialist for Atomic Engineering during the 1970s. During his work he educated himself on current research in the field and seeing the troublesome research he decided to conduct his own (Elliston et al., 1985, p. 119). His research argued that the management philosophies of the nuclear industry did not develop to include ethical or safety questions, and were narrowly defined (Elliston et al., 1985, p. 120). This paper would later be submitted to the *Congressional Record* and used to testify in front of Congress (Elliston et al., 1985, p. 118).

To do this, he gathered allies. At first he allied with William Seymour, an environmental specialist who helped with the research and in getting the paper published (Elliston et al., 1985, p. 120). He then allied with Bruce Arnold who often represented Friends of the Earth, an environmental organization (Elliston et al., 1985, p. 118). Arnold used Thomas's paper to testify in front of Congress and warn of the dangers of nuclear energy (Elliston et al., 1985, p. 118). After these efforts, Thomas then leaked to the press about the subject to try and raise awareness of the issues.

William Sanjour's resistance would lead to the Supreme Court's decision in Sanjour v EPA in which it was decided that public employees "have a right to speak to environmental community groups" under the First Amendment (National Whistleblower Center). This decision strengthened future resistance efforts by bureaucrats. Sanjour, having worked for the EPA for 20 years, was given the choice between being a "good soldier" who followed orders and a "good citizen" who obeyed the law. As Sanjour stated: "I have not, I'm afraid, been a very good soldier" (Sanjour, 1995). In charge of enacting the Resource Conservation and Recovery Act (RCRA) concerning toxic waste, he would inform his superiors at the EPA about the need to meet RCRA legal deadlines; they laughed, and removed him from the job. Emboldened, Sanjour contacted an environmental organization that sued the EPA into compliance.

Without this relationship, Sanjour's resistance effort would have been all but doomed. Having powerful counterweights outside of the organization can provide legitimacy and strengthen one's position vis-à-vis unjust practices of the organization.

Peter Scranton, a regional director for the EPA during the 1970s, recognized that a chemical crisis occurred when excess chemicals had to be moved and stored at other regional locations, triggering a situation in which those chemicals had a chance of leaking into the local area, poisoning the surrounding environment. Scranton's office was targeted, and as a "scrappy individual, [who] believed in protecting the environment at all costs," he would not agree to a transfer (Elliston et al., 1985, p. 44). He attempted to go through internal channels to remedy the situation, but that effort failed (Elliston et al., 1985, p. 46). Scranton turned to one of the few allies he had left – Evelyn Fullerton, a leading activist in the Sierra Club (Elliston et al., 1985, p. 47). This created local attention and a public outcry. That external pressure caused the chemicals to be transferred elsewhere, and the community was spared a future environmental catastrophe. Without ties to independent organizations, journalists and other influential actors, his opposition to a dangerous chemical transfer may have resulted in a tragic situation.

Jefferson Smith was a foreign service officer for the Department of State. In 2016 he received the Rivkin Award for constructive dissent by a mid-career officer ("2016 Constructive Dissent," 2016). He highlighted the issue of wage and worker inequalities at US embassies and how such practices should be changed to empower workers, not exploit them ("2016 Constructive Dissent," 2016). He was posted to Kuwait at the time and presented his evidence at a regional managers' conference, earning allies for the issue ("2016 Constructive Dissent," 2016). With these allies he wrote a cable to Washington, signed by six regional ambassadors, proposing new compensation standards for locally employed staff ("2016 Constructive Dissent," 2016). Smith won a better compensation package for the region and helped address unjust practices. Without those signatures and his thorough research, his initiative would have been likely to fail.

ALERT DECISION-MAKERS

An obvious and initial step is to raise the issue with the person most involved in the injustice. There are both practical and altruistic reasons for doing this. Practically speaking, the injustice may be perpetuated by the individual because they may believe nobody is noticing, or that they will not be caught. While formally "catching" them and punishing them may be difficult, confronting them directly about the injustice can break down the defensive barriers they may have constructed concerning the act. Once people know, the individual may stop the act all together. Another practical reason is categorical. If the resistor confronts the individual about the injustice and the injustice persists, then it clarifies the issue as being purposeful, as opposed to accidental. A last practical reason for confronting the issue directly with the person is that it also can provide legal cover in the forms of "building a case" that may go as far as a legal confrontation. The injustice may be happening accidently, and merely informing the individual of the wrongdoing may stop it altogether.

Simply talking to your supervisor is another option at a lower temperature, so to speak. The supervisor may be open-minded and help the resistor in remedying the problem. However, talking to the supervisor may also create considerable problems. For instance, if the supervisor is part of the problem, then confronting them could lead to retaliation. However, if the supervisor is supportive and recognizes the issue as such, then an avenue of reform is created. A procedural caution: in many organizations an individual that sees corruption or other abuses and wishes to remedy the abuse has to go through the internal organization before externally blowing the whistle, and must do so to secure legal protections.

When the supervisor is unresponsive or is perpetuating the abuse, an option is to go "over their head" and talk to the "higher-ups." This move can be poignant for a variety of reasons. First, it shows the resolve of the resistor. The issue becomes not just a bureaucrat becoming aware of an issue and keeping it within the immediate group involved, but rather a line bureaucrat elevating the issue so as to involve key decision-makers. This strategy also provides a legal "paper trail" and helps the resistor build their case against not only the individuals involved, but against the organization generally. This is especially the case if the executive positions are colluding in the abuses.

There are some cautions that the potential resistor should keep in mind. Informing superiors of policy recommendations can often invite reprisals.

Some organizations have specific policies against such practices and by breaking the chain-of-command the resistor opens themselves up to retaliation and outright termination. Another caution to keep in mind is that the higher one goes up the hierarchy when raising an issue, the worse the retaliation may actually become.

The Rivkin Award is one of four "constructive dissent awards" offered by the Department of State. The others are: the Harris Award for Foreign Service

Specialists; Harriman Award for entry-level officers, and the Herter Award for Senior Foreign Service ("2016 Constructive Dissent," 2016).

- Theodore Lyng was a Foreign Service Officer in the Department of State. In 2013, he received the Rivkin Award for mid-level foreign service employees who exercised meaningful dissent (Taylor, 2013). The issue he raised concerned a State Department policy of directly dealing with only liberal or moderate Muslim leaders in Indonesia (Taylor, 2013). He successfully recommended to his supervisors, and lobbied for, the integration of conservative Muslim leaders in the discussion; otherwise, it would be simply "preaching to the choir" (Taylor, 2013).
- James Rider received the Harriman Award for constructive dissent in 2013. Rider noticed a legal loophole that allowed children of US parents who were citizens to obtain US passports for their children when neither child nor parents spent any meaningful time in the US (Taylor, 2013). According to the American Foreign Service Association, Rider brought up an inconsistency where these same children would not have received a passport if they applied in the US, but did receive one for applying outside of the US (Taylor, 2013). Correcting this discrepancy was in the interests of the State Department and his going to his supervisor remedied the situation.
- Having won the award and having helped to change policy, Lyng and Rider have served as good examples of what simply talking to one's supervisor can yield. Of course, the Department of State may be blessed with a unique culture of dissent, so this behavior is more tolerated, but all potential resistors should consider speaking to the supervisor about the perceived issue. The resistor may be pleasantly surprised by a positive response to addressing the issue.

Coleen Rowley a special agent for the FBI, identified information showing failures in the FBI prior to 9/11 (Staff, National Whistleblower Center (2017a)) She brought that information to the attention of FBI Director Robert Mueller, which prompted an investigation into the matter and earned her designation as TIME Person of the Year (Staff, Government Accountability Project, 2017b). Later, in 2003, she would attempt to prevent the invasion of Iraq by warning the director and other superiors who had authority concerning the situation (Staff, Government Accountability Project, 2017b). That effort was unsuccessful, but she retired in protest and went on to present talks concerning ethics and civil liberties.

Margaret Clinton was a senior information scientist at the Chicago Municipal Health Planning Council. She was tasked with managing various computer programs and databases. An issue arose when she was tasked to create an Accounts Payable System (ACPAS) which helped manage the increasing levels of paperwork hospitals had to administer, and the Patient Monitoring System (PAMOS) which was an emergency monitoring system for patients and nurses (Elliston et al., 1985, p. 68). These systems worked well separately, but management asked to combine the two into one large system (Elliston et al., 1985, p. 69). It was in Elliston's professional opinion that combining the two systems would create unnecessary slowdowns, worsening response times and thereby creating a risk for patients and possible loss of life (Elliston et al., 1985, p. 69). She went to professional organizations, such as the Institute of Electrical and Electronics Engineers (IEEE), which supported her professional stance. Clinton attempted to use this leverage with her supervisors and superiors, but would be terminated for breaking the chain of command (Elliston et al., 1985, p. 73). Her efforts eventually prevented the policy from being enacted, but she suffered great personal costs.

Philip Ryther was an evaluation chief of the Federal Aviation Administration (FAA) and would be forced into retirement after 26 years of service (Nader, Petkas and Blackwell, 1972. p. 177). In 1970 he filed a report critical of air charter abuses and the applicable FAA regulations, making recommendations to remedy the poor policy. Ryther received little access from his superiors, so he bypassed channels and talked to the deputy administrator. The report would be generally ignored until the tragic accident of a plane crash that would take the lives of Wichita State University's football team on October 2, 1970 (Nader, Petkas and Blackwell, 1972, p. 177). After the plane crash, he held that it never would have occurred if his recommendations had been adopted. Management finally adopted and implemented his policies after the tragedy. However, in this case Ryther, while getting his policies implemented by informing staff as to the tragedy supporting his stance, lost his job in the process.

COMMUNICATE ALERTS THROUGH SPECIAL CHANNELS

Some agencies have hotlines for employees to alert the organization about potential abuses, inefficiencies or criminal activity. Hotlines typically also aim to maintain anonymity for the resistor. While a simple form of resistance, this does create a record of the incident and can be referenced later if the situation were to escalate. Hotlines can also be coupled with persistence. A single call may equate to little change, but repeated calls about various abuses over the course of months or even years can elicit meaningful responses from the organization. A powerful step a resistor should consider taking is the utilization of the Office of Inspector General (OIG). The office is built specifically for dissenters and whistleblowers who need to voice concerns and complaints about abuse and fraud in their organizations. It is their natural ally. The OIG will help facilitate lawsuits, and investigations have become more supportive of whistleblowers. Many departments and agencies have some sort of OIG as a lightning rod for dissent. Contacting the headquarters of the organization is another strategy that can help in the resistance effort.

An example is the Department of State's Dissent Channel. This channel was created as a way for lower level foreign service officers to have a direct line to executives and State Department headquarters. A response may be mandated within a certain period of time. This mandate, coupled with persistence, can lead to a powerful resistance effort in which the organization knows where the resistor stands, and that the resistor is not fading away.

Contacting headquarters is the ultimate internal mechanism of change. But if that proves to be a dead end, if the organization is unwilling or unable to fix the particular problem, then addressing the problem may have to be an external effort.

Tom Reay was a soldier stationed on the *USS Fulton*, which was a repair ship. He was in charge of the Division of Electronic Repairs, and noticed cost overruns (Johnson, 2003, p. 6). Reay decided to go to outside distributors to buy the parts for much less, and logged the money saved (Johnson, 2003, p. 6). Specifically, lightbulbs were being purchased for $18 each until Reay found distributors that sold them for 15 cents each (Johnson, 2003, p. 7). He began to call the Department of Defense hotline every week to report the matter, but little developed. After he left the service he would receive an unexpected package with a monetary reward for his "lightbulb suggestion" (Johnson, 2003, p. 7).

While an almost naively simple example of using department hotlines, this strategy is important to keep in mind due to its simplicity. Hotlines have grown in popularity and using them can be a "suggestion box" for change. They also create a record and reputation of thoughtfulness concerning the organization.

Nancy Kusen was an administrative contracting officer in the Department of Defense and attempted to use the hotline, but suffered retaliation. Specifically, she worked for the Defense Logistics Agency, Defense Contract Administration Services Management Area (DCASMA). Kusen noticed contract discrepancies and attempted to report the issue through internal channels (Johnson, 2003, p. 7). When those failed she leaked the story to the press, and found success in outside group support (Johnson, 2003, p. 8). The outside organization, U.S. Price Fighter Detachment, ran a "should cost" report to lend weight to Kusen's claims, finding that the Department of Defense were being overcharged by hundreds of thousands of dollars (Johnson, 2003, p. 8). Kusen would gain promotion, those officials who retaliated against her lost their jobs, and she was vindicated.

Frederic Whitehurst was a chemist and lab supervisor for the FBI's crime lab (Staff, CNN 1998). He was the leading bomb residue expert and carried considerable weight in the lab. Whitehurst would attempt to reform the crime lab by contacting headquarters over the course of ten years, discussing the faulty work and poor practices of the lab (Staff, CNN 1998). His criticisms did lead to reform of the lab, but encountered retaliation and an FBI investigation (Staff, CNN, 1998). He received $1.166 million in compensation for the retaliation and retired soon after (Staff, CNN, 1998).

Contacting headquarters may not be a quick fix, but it can have an effect if one is persistent. It is up to the individual to gauge their patience, persistence and power in contacting headquarters.

TRANSFER OFFICES (OR NOT)

A relatively passive form of resistance is to ask for a transfer to a different office or department. This transfer can slow or block the implementation of abusive policy if the resistor is central to the policy implementation. Transferring offices is often granted given the difficulty of firing public servants. Transferring is also symbolic of free-market concepts of "voting with your feet." If a new policy is launched, but staff signal their resistance by requesting transfers, then it is a signal to management and executives that the policy may be objectionable.

While transferring offices may be a form of resistance, so is purposefully not transferring offices. There are unique advantages to "staying put" in one's position as long as possible during a resistance effort. The position may provide unique information and access to nuanced understandings of the abuse. Management, knowing this, may aim to forcibly transfer the resistor from such a position. Staying in one's position can be emboldening to subordinates and serve as a general morale booster to those who may wish to join the resistance efforts.

To resist the transfer may be an escalation of the situation. Management may escalate further to legal, personal or professional retaliation. The organization may forcibly transfer the resistor, and the only possible counter may be legal action. Knowing one's rights and protections becomes critical.

The case of Shawn "Spiderman" Carpenter is a particularly noble instance of refusing an office transfer. He was a computer hacker for an independent contractor named Sandia. Upon discovering an elite Chinese hacking group named "Titan Rain," he would refuse any transfers and use the information from Sandia to become an informant for Army intelligence officers and the FBI (Staff, TIME, 2005). Carpenter would eventually be discovered by Sandia, and fired (Staff, TIME, 2005). He was able to join another defense contractor doing similar work. Without his work as an informant, foreign hackers could have compromised national security. He resisted his private sector organization, not for private gain or individual malice toward superiors, but in the interest of the country.

Franz Gayl served in the military from the age of 17. He was a science adviser at the Pentagon tasked to find policy recommendations (Staff, Government Accountability Project, 2017b). Gayl found that there were an insufficient number of MRAPs (Mine Resistant Ambush Protected Vehicles) in response to IED (Improvised Explosive Device) explosions Staff, Government Accountability Project, 2017b). His policy recommendation, more MRAPS rather than Humvees, was lost in the bureaucracy. In response, he would attempt to give a presentation on the subject, but would be blocked by management. Gayl suffered retaliation for his persistence in the form of a job description change to limit his ability to research, but he refused to fulfill his new job description and conducted research anyway. He would use his office to later leak his findings to the press, causing a firestorm. The result was political and public attention on the issue and investigations into the matter. Most importantly, the emphasis on deploying MRAPs saved thousands of lives ("Franz Gayl," n.d.).

Lieutenant Colonel Darrel Vandeveld has had a distinguished career in the US Army, receiving a Bronze Star Medal, Iraqi Campaign Medal, Joint Service Commendation Medal, and two Joint Meritorious Unit Awards (Staff, National Whistleblower Center, 2017c). He was the prosecutor at the Office of Military Commissions in Guantanamo Bay, Cuba, where he observed "serious violations," including "abusive interrogations, evidence withheld from the defense, and judicial incompetence" (Staff, National Whistleblower Center, 2017c). With these horrors in mind, he found it unethical and legally untenable to prosecute Mohammad Jawad (Staff, National Whistleblower Center, 2017c). His transfer from Jawad's case slowed the process of wrongful legal action, but helped call attention to the need for reform and justice.

RESIGN IN PROTEST

An effective strategy may be to simply resign. One can resign loudly, or resign quietly. Resigning as a form of resistance operates on the notion that to implement policy, politicians and management need experts on the ground who know the situation. If the experts were to resign, policy implementation might become difficult.

Resigning quietly can provide better legal cover and generally mitigate the amount of damage a resistor may suffer from disgruntled management. Conversely, a loud resignation can multiply the damage done to an agency, but can also increase the risk of retaliation from management. "Loud resignation" is the act of not only resigning, but making the effort to state to the public or press why the resignation is occurring, the injustices that may be occurring, and even policy recommendations. "Loud resignation" can be shaped in a variety of different ways. It can be professional criticism, moral criticism or outright assault on the agency. Of course, one can only resign once from an agency, so it should be done with considerable thought.

There is also the symbolic aspect of quitting an unjust organization. For example, the Environmental Protection Agency does not have a monopoly on environmental advocacy, policy or expertise. Many outside organizations, from Greenpeace to the Sierra Club, provide knowledge, advocacy and recommendations for many of the world's most pressing environmental issues. If a bureaucrat from the EPA notices injustice and wishes to separate from the abuse, a simple solution would be to leave and join other environmental organizations. This disassociation can give the resistor a strong background for further resistance.

Hal Freeman was the Regional Manager in the Office of Civil Rights in San Francisco. He loudly resigned after discovering policies of discrimination against individuals with AIDS or suspected of having AIDS (Johnson, 2003, p. 63). Given his high status in the administration and the reason for his exit, his resignation caught the attention of the country. He coupled his resignation with a simple solution – individuals with AIDS or suspected of having AIDS are a protected class and their rights need to be enforced (Johnson, 2003, p. 63). The fact of his resignation, the simplicity of his policy recommendation, and the seriousness of the AIDS epidemic at the time gave him support among the press, human rights groups and politicians. His resignation was a catalyst that provoked change and would be successful. Administrative improvements happened almost immediately, which included new coordinators, outreach programs, and publications explaining individual rights.

Freeman benefited from his position in the administration, but the average bureaucrat can also utilize resignation as a tool. Many bureaucrats leave the government with little attention. When one loudly resigns, it can elevate their status, especially if the bureaucrat is a respected professional with deep expertise (Cimons, 1986).

William Stieglitz worked for the National Highway Safety Bureau before loudly resigning in 1967 upon discovery that his recommendations to strengthen safety standards were almost completely ignored (Nader, Petkas and Blackwell, 1972, p. 99). His resignation, the day after the standards were made public, would eventually force a strengthening of the standards.

Stieglitz spent much of his life studying safety standards in the Air Force, lecturing at Princeton, and advising the predecessor of NASA, the National Advisory Commission for Aeronautics (Nader, Petkas and Blackwell, 1972, p. 100). He would transition to automobile safety and became a leading expert who helped study and produce automobile safety standards in 1967. However, agencies ignored his suggestions and produced weak standards. He resigned, testified to Congress and provided specific counterpoints and policies to issues concerning the standards. Stieglitz was successful in strengthening the standards (Staff, CQ Almanac, 1967).

REFUSE ILLEGAL ORDERS

Illegal orders or criminal behavior on behalf of an individual or an organization is particularly heinous and ought to be resisted. Conducting illegal activity is typically considered morally wrong. Following oaths of office and ethics guidelines, bureaucrats as public servants should not act as organizational automatons who unquestionably carry out orders. They must be conscious of what the orders demand of them and how such actions may adversely affect the law, the citizenry and themselves.

Resisting such behavior can contribute to the legitimacy of the resistance movement. While resistance that is concerned with policy differences can lessen legitimacy simply because the resistor does not "agree" with the policy or its implementation, resisting orders that ask the bureaucrat to conduct illegal activity, or bringing to light criminal behavior that a coworker has committed, is something that many people would enthusiastically support.

Charles Pettis was an engineer in Peru for Brown and Root Overseas Inc., working on a $47 million project to build a road across the Andes. This infrastructure project was funded by USAID and the Export-Import Bank. He was tasked to both represent the client, the Peruvian government, and to maintain engineering standards outlined in the contract (Nader, Petkas and Blackwell, 1972, p. 135). Pettis found structural deficiencies in the plans and warned that it would ultimately lead to the death of people during a landslide, a common situation in the Andes Mountain region (Nader, Petkas and Blackwell, 1972, p. 136). In fact, 31 deaths later resulted from the very situation he was trying to prevent. He suggested ways of remedying, compensating and otherwise addressing the issues involved with the faulty construction project, but the company retaliated. It replaced him, slandered him, and would fire him in 1968. Later, Pettis contacted Senator Proxmire's staff and they set up an appointment with the Government Accountability Office (GAO) (Nader, Petkas and Blackwell, 1972, p. 138). A report was compiled and released in 1971, confirming Pettis's allegations concerning mismanagement and corruption. Brown and Root Overseas Inc. lost the contract and the construction was turned over to the Peruvian government.

Pettis resisted the illegal actions of Brown and Root Overseas Inc. concerning contract fulfillment, and endangering human lives. Without his resistance, the construction project may never have been stopped and more lives could have been lost.

LEAK INFORMATION

A potent avenue of bureaucratic resistance is to leak information to the press or supporting organizations. Public scrutiny is important to most government functioning and is considered a normative value by most developed democratic standards. While the danger may be high when leaking information to the public, the benefits can add a multiplying effect to the resistance effort.

"Ghostwriting," typically by an insider, is the act of remaining anonymous while using the on-the-job information and access to "inside" information in order to write inflammatory exposures of the organization. "Ghostwriting" is an active exercise in which the individual aims to stay under cover while purposefully highlighting the abuses in question. This tactic is similar to "leaking information," but with the added step of crafting the message, not merely supplying the content. Many news articles cite "unauthorized" or "anonymous sources" that provide damaging testimony, ghostwrite, or otherwise seek outside outlets to voice dissent. Resistors must exercise caution in when, how and the general method they use to write and submit their letters and testimony.

When going internally through an organization pressures can build from direct supervisors, colleagues and higher-ups. When vested interests gain from the injustice being committed, the bureaucrat must go outside of the organization to shine light on the issue. Public scrutiny is important to most government functioning and is considered a normative value by most developed democratic standards. In the following examples, the historical precedence and benefits are shown.

Benjamin Franklin was many things – diplomat, scientist and inventor – but "leaker" is rarely included on the list of leakers. In 1772, however, Franklin released confidential letters between the British monarchy and Massachusetts Governor Hutchinson. This leak to Adam Cushing, the Speaker of the Massachusetts Assembly, helped foment the American Revolution by fueling animosity between the British government and American colonies (Smith, 2013). Franklin would admit publicly, on December 25, 1773, to be the leaker of the letter, an action that led him to be labeled as an "incendiary agent" by the Privy Council on January 19, 1774 (Smith, 2013). The letters contained evidence suggesting that Governor Hutchinson was feeding "bad advice" purposefully to British officials in Boston, fueling animosities within the city (Smith, 2013). Given that, at the time, blame was being largely placed on the American legislators for the dysfunction between Boston and Britain, the revelation of the letters allowed for public scrutiny and for the truth to be known.

The famous 1972 Watergate scandal centered on "Deep Throat," revealed only decades later to have been Mark Felt, a high official in the FBI, whose persistent leaking of the Nixon Administration's transgressions brought down the president. Felt met reporters in parking garages at night, put out flower pots to signal stories, and ultimately stayed hidden from the public view. Utilizing his experience as an anti-Nazi spy hunter, he would strike quietly and effectively against the Nixon Administration by confirming and giving context to *Washington Post* stories (Von Drehle, 2005) by Bob Woodward and Carl Bernstein. Given Nixon's history of ruthless lawbreaking, there was no caution that was too great (Von Drehle, 2005).

Robert Kelly was an agricultural pesticide research scientist for the Virginia Farm and Produce Agency (FPA) during the 1970s. His case concerning the carcinogen "onozine" in apple production is an ironic "case-and-point" with the frustrating realities of internal resistance. He submitted critiques and policy corrections concerning another chemical "nevrin" which was being sprayed onto cornfields. He would, for five years, use internal channels to try to stop the use of nevrin. However, his information as to the dangers of nevrin leaked to the press, and his work was declared superfluous and irrelevant to the discussion (Elliston et al., 1985, p. 56). Kelly became disillusioned with internal channels (Elliston et al., 1985, p. 56).

When onozine was discovered, he wasted little time with internal channels. He went directly to the press (*The Richmond Herald*) to break the story on the dangerous chemical. News spread like wildfire and NBC asked for an interview (Elliston et al., 1985, p. 62). Press attention led to policy changes on the use of onozine, and Kelly achieved more through the press in less than a year than he had in "six years of writing memos" (Elliston et al., 1985, p. 64).

Peter Buxtun, a venereal disease investigator for the U.S. Public Health Service in San Francisco, uncovered the "Untreated Syphilis in the Male Negro" Tuskegee Study in 1966. Prompted by budget cuts in 1932 during the Great Depression, the government decided to study untreated cases of syphilis in 400 "volunteers" in the African American community, but without following ethical guidelines or offering treatment to the participants in the study. Buxtun would leak his findings to *The Washington Star* in 1972. Having come from Nazi Germany as a refugee, Buxton drew "disturbing similarities" between the Tuskegee Study and the 1947 Nuremberg Doctors' Trial (Kerr and Rivero, 2014). Once this news reached the press, senators and the public were outraged. This prompted intergovernmental oversight and accountability. President Bill Clinton would apologize in 1997 and the survivors would receive $10 million in compensation subsequent to a lawsuit (Kerr and Rivero, 2014).

PETITION

Petition is an effective tactic that can highlight the scope of the resistance as well as its solidarity. Depending on the issue, the relevance and the number of signatures, petitions can provide a meaningful, democratic and public way of expressing bureaucratic resistance to orders that are judged to be illegitimate.

Petitions are typically documents with a statement of grievance that may contain a policy recommendation, and are typically thought of as being signed by hundreds or thousands of citizens as a protest against perceived abuses. But they may also be initiated by bureaucrats as a protest against poor policy. Writing a strongly worded letter with signatures should not be the sole reliance of a bureaucratic resistance effort. But such measures are helpful as an escalatory tactic if the abuse is not remedied in other ways.

Shortly after the birth of the United States, dissenters began to differ with the new American leadership. While this is not surprising, the story of Samuel Shaw, Richard Marven and John Grannis is surprising. In 1777, a secret meeting was held on the warship *Warren* to oppose the autocratic rule of Commander of the Continental Navy, Commodore Esek Hopkins. The group of ten dissenters would sign a petition and present it to Congress, telling of the abuses of Hopkins, and how he tortured British troops (Kohn, 2011).

Hopkins would file a libel lawsuit against the dissenters in which Marven and Shaw were put in jail. But Hopkins's retaliation was short-lived. Congress would pass the country's first whistleblower protection laws protecting those who wish to give information to the Congress concerning "misconduct, frauds, or misdemeanors committed by any officers or persons in the service" (Kohn, 2011). Congress would also pass provisions covering the dissenters' legal fees against Hopkins. This case would help create the culture of dissent in the US and is one of the predecessors of many whistleblower protection laws and rulings.

Leon Panetta (who later became Chief of Staff in the White House and Secretary of Defense) was fired from Office of Civil Rights in Department of Health, Education, and Wellness (HEW) in 1970. His colleagues at HEW would essentially rebel. They signed a petition of almost 2,000 signatures to Secretary Robert H. Finch. Finch capitulated and agreed to discuss the matter with HEW staff. Unsatisfied with that, Peter Gall, a special assistant for press relations to Panetta, initiated a letter (signed by 125 people) to President Nixon (Nader, Petkas and Blackwell, 1972, p. 171). Subsequent to the letter, he publicly resigned and wrote to *The Washington Monthly* voicing criticism of the Administration.

Petitions matter and add voice to a singular resistor's efforts. In this case the HEW staff caught the attention of Secretary Finch, and thereby publicly raised an important issue concerning the Administration's role (or lack thereof) in civil rights policy.

BLOW THE WHISTLE

Whistleblowing is a collection of strategies that generally involve going outside of the organization, voicing concerns loudly to the public, and often incorporating the legislature or other organizations. Formal whistleblowing can take years to have its full impact. There is a difference between acting internally to remedy abuse, and acting externally in a vociferous manner and with the intent to destroy.

Going on the offensive can grab headlines, establish more of a sense of sincerity, and unequivocally state who is to blame, for what problem, and for the immorality of it all. This quickly creates an "us versus them" mentality that becomes obvious. Becoming loud and direct with one's criticism also can elevate the individual to a "celebrity status" in which the news follows him or her, what they say, and what may happen to them. The resistor can become the spokesperson for the issue. For example, if the celebrity resistor is terminated for his or her opposition, the news will probably report it in terms favorable to the resistor.

However, such notoriety can bury the message, wherein the issue is lost and the controversy is about the resistor, not the issue itself. With celebrity status, an "all out war" can occur with anonymous threats to oneself and family, smear campaigns, and extensive legal assaults. Essentially, if one is going to resist loudly and unequivocally, one ought to be prepared in every possible way.

The cases below highlight the effects of publicly blasting the head of an agency or the agency itself. Whistleblowing is a collection of strategies that generally involve going outside of the organization, voicing concerns loudly to the public, and often incorporating the support of legislators or other organizations. Formal whistleblowing can take years to have its full impact.

Stanley Adams became a formal whistleblower after giving the European Economic Community (EEC), and cooperating with the EEC, information to investigate Swiss pharmaceutical company Roche (Staff, theguardian, 2001). At the time Adams worked for Roche, and had access to incriminating documents regarding price fixing between Roche and 12 other companies (Staff, theguardian, 2001). His whistleblowing extended over a period of three decades before any legal actions were delivered – a record fine of 523 million pounds.

Adams' case is an example of a formal whistleblowing experience for several reasons. He was in the organization, and voiced his concerns externally, providing confidential information to authorities. He suffered retaliation, which is common in whistleblowing cases. His success was due to external pressures on the organization, and without his information the investigation may have never been initiated.

Clive Ponting was a civil servant at the British Ministry of Defence in 1984 (Malnick, 2014). He became an official whistleblower when he decided to leak documents related to the tragic sinking of the Argentine battleship *Belgrano* (Malnick, 2014) during the Falkland war with Argentina. Interestingly, Prime Minister Margaret Thatcher would defend Ponting, recommending that the officials "not be too harsh" in punishing him (Malnick, 2014). He would receive his salary and be reinstated after Thatcher's intervention. Without Thatcher's unsolicited intervention, Ponting would more than likely have lost his job and benefits. With Thatcher's intervention, he resisted and suffered almost no reprisals.

In the case of Ernest Fitzgerald, lawsuits won him hundreds of thousands of dollars in damages and compensation while bringing to light large cost overruns on Pentagon contracts. He would also use Congressional testimony to publicly describe the abuses within the Pentagon, earning him the status of "the most hated person in the Airforce" (Carlson, 1985).

In 1968 Fitzgerald exposed millions of dollars of cost overruns charged to the Pentagon, from hours worked to toilet seats. After going public, Fitzgerald was fired. He would sue the Air Force twice for reinstatement. He would even sue President Nixon for "violating his constitutional rights," reaching a settlement of $142,000 (Carlson, 1985). His success in court gave him notoriety in the field, and his impeccable expertise at exposing waste gave him credibility on the issues. He was not publicly deriding the Pentagon with hearsay information, but rather validating the cost overruns, making allies, and acting impeccably in his execution. In his savagery, he was sophisticated.

Fitzgerald's actions involved blowing the whistle during a Congressional hearing on the C-5A transport plane. The C-5A would come in at $2 billion over budget, and in Congressional testimony the Pentagon tried to plead ignorance of any wrongdoing. He would refer to himself sarcastically as the "only bureaucrat in the world suing for more work" (Carlson, 1985). This attitude, aptitude and aspiration would bring him the title of "folk hero of federal employees" from the *New York Times* (Carlson, 1985).

LAWYER UP

Given the potential for retaliation, "lawyering up" is an obligatory step for any whistleblower speaking up against unjust practices. Knowing one's rights as an employee and whistleblower is critical. "Lawyering up" bears costs, and should be calculated by any potential whistleblower. In many cases, litigation can last for years, and a long series of lawsuits can lead to financial stress and even health problems.

Filing a lawsuit affords leverage to the whistleblower by using the law to advance the interests of the public and to remedy wrongful conduct. For example, legal pathways for resistance include the Whistleblower Protection Act of 1978, health and safety acts such as the Clean Water Act of 1972, and the False Claims Act of 1863. Multiple lawsuits may need to be filed in response to different forms of retaliation.

Supporting organizations may well bear the entire cost of litigation and lend "weight" to an issue. Without such support, an individual could be labeled as a "lone zealot." The more support the better, and the courtroom may well be the "battleground."

Robert Olsen was a Foreign Service Officer stationed in Sao Paulo (Staff, New York Times, 1998). He was terminated after not following "profiles" that were later deemed racist by a federal court (Staff, New York Times, 1998). These profiles included acronyms such as "LP" for "looks poor," "TP" for "talks poor" and "LR" for "looks rough" (Staff, New York Times, 1998). Those labels were primarily assigned to minority groups (Staff, New York Times, 1998). After his dismissal. Olsen sued and won back his position.

Legal action is involved in many resistance or whistleblowing experiences. When one resists laws, or attempts to enforce laws, or suffers reprisals, resistors need to know their protections, and legal action is necessary to many efforts. Although not all situations end up in court, the resistor should always consider the possibility that using a lawyer may help the cause. In Olsen's case, legal action helped remedy the issue; in other cases, legal action is insufficient.

When large lawsuits make the press, one can imagine it is almost impossible to maintain anonymity. However, the resistor can often maintain secrecy. In the case of Harbinger Capital Partners, an anonymous whistleblower filed a suit in 2015 alleging that Harbinger Capital Partners, owned by Philip Falcone, who is notorious for making billions from the collapse of the housing market, did not pay New York state taxes from 2004 to 2009 (Goldstein, 2017). The anonymous whistleblower used the False Claims Act, and received $8.8 million from the successful lawsuit (Goldstein, 2017).

There are many laws and regulations one can sue over. The False Claims Act is particularly lucrative given the large payouts that can occur, but the potential resistor should not be lulled into this single strategy. Lawsuits cost money, and time. While many times their verdicts are final and backed by the powerful force of law, losing lawsuits can also be costly, creating hardship and little change in the process.

Marsha Coleman-Adebayo was a Senior Policy Analyst in the Office of Administrator at the US Environmental Protection Agency. She would sue the EPA on the basis of race, sex and hostile work environment in 2000 (Dr. Marsha Coleman-Adebayo Biography, 2017). Coleman-Adebayo would succeed in her lawsuit, leading to the formulation of The No FEAR Act (Notification of Federal Employee Antidiscrimination and Retaliation Act of 2002). That act created the mandate that at the end of a fiscal year each federal agency must submit a report outlining the discrimination cases ongoing, the amount of reimbursement costs, the number of disciplinary actions and their relevant policy context, causal analysis, and any actions planned or taken to improve compliance or civil rights programs of the agency (No FEAR Act of 2002. P.L. 107-174. 107th Congress) (2002).

Coleman-Adebayo created outside organizations to support resistors in organizations who aimed to hold government accountable, especially to the standards concerning civil rights. These organizations, The No FEAR Institute and The No FEAR Coalition, helped inform and shape dialogue on the issues surrounding federal employees and dissent both domestically and internationally (Dr. Marsha Coleman-Adebayo Biography, 2017).

Trudi Lytle, a 4th grade teacher at Earl Elementary in the Clark County Public School District (CCSD) in Nevada relied entirely on the courts to remedy her whistleblower complaints and to handle the subsequent retaliation she endured. Her efforts largely failed, contributing to a decline in her "physical and psychological well-being" and creating "feelings of isolation and powerlessness" (Miethe, 1999, p. 170).

For the 1991–92 academic year the CCSD implemented the SOAR (Student Options for Academic Realization) Program. SOAR was meant to give special priority to "gifted" students with smaller class sizes and bonus funding (Miethe, 1999, p. 165). However, the classroom was largely filled with teachers' and principals' children (Miethe, 1999, p. 165). SOAR was essentially the manipulation of public funds and policy to better the private interests of public administrators within the system. Lytle, rejecting this injustice, blew the whistle by writing a letter to a Las Vegas newspaper criticizing the program and highlighting important issues that ought to be addressed. She would suffer retaliation for voicing her First Amendment rights; Lytle was transferred to different classes at different schools and letters criticizing her performance were placed in her file (Miethe, 1999, pp. 167–8).

To counter this retaliation, she turned primarily to the law. Lytle hired an attorney and filed a civil rights suit against the principal, administrators and CCSD for "intentionally depriving her of substantive and procedural due process rights" (Miethe, 1999, p. 168). That strategy would be largely unsuccessful. Although her lawsuit found that she should be reinstated at Earl Elementary, the school's authority as to placement was maintained (Rashke, 2015).

TAKEAWAYS

- "Willful blindness" can result in organizational disasters.
- Ethical dissent can be effective in preventing or correcting corrupt policies and procedures.

- Public employees at all levels need to be involved in meaningful problem solving to head off ethical transgressions.
- Strategies for quiet resistance or constructive dissent are available.
- "Blowing the whistle" does not necessarily mean "blowing your job."

SELECTIONS FOR FURTHER READING AND RESEARCH

Johnson, R.A. (2003) *Whistle-blowing: When It Works and Why*. London: Lynne Rienner Publishers.
Considers how resisters choose to blow the whistle.

National Whistleblower Center. https://www.whistleblowers.org
Highlights the difficulties of being a whistleblower, and supports their efforts to counter illegal and unethical situations.

O'Leary, R. (2019) The Ethics of Dissent: Managing Guerilla Government. Third edition. Thousand Oaks, CA: Sage.
Advises public servants about safely navigating bureaucratic-democratic tensions in the context of organizational behaviors that require ethical responses.

Public Integrity.
International journal publishing research on ethical issues in public administration, such as corruption, social equity, law, criminal justice and human rights.

https://www.tandfonline.com/journals
Peer-reviewed journal publishing research on ethical issues in public administration, such as corruption, social equity, law, criminal justice and human rights.

Weisband, E. and Franck, T.M. (1975) *Resignation in Protest: Political and Ethical Choices between Loyalty to Team and Loyalty to Conscience in American Public Life*. New York: Grossman Publishers.
Addresses conflicts that senior public officials may encounter between team loyalty and personal conscience.

REFERENCES

Berlinski, Claire (2016, May 11) Did Britain fall into Putin's trap in prosecuting a Russian dissident. *National Review*. http://www.nationalreview.com/article/435238/ussian-dissident-vladimir-bukovsky-sues-uk-government-libel
Bumiller, Elisabeth and Dao, James (2011, November 8) Air Force officials disciplined over handling of human remains. *New York Times*. http://www.nytimes.com/2011/11/09/us/senior-air-force-officials-disciplined-over-handling-of-human-remains.html
Carlson, Peter (1985, December 9) A. Ernest Fitzgerald. *People*. http://people.com/archive/a-ernest-fitzgerald-vol-24-no-24/

Cimons, Marlene (1986, February 22) U.S. rights aide charges gay bias, Quits. *Los Angeles Times.* http://articles.latimes.com/1986-02-22/local/me-10597_1_civil -rights

Cushman, John H. Jr. (1998, May 11) Ronald Ridenhour, 52, veteran who reported My Lai massacre. *New York Times.* http://www.nytimes.com/1998/05/11/us/ronald -ridenhour-52-veteran-who-reported-my-lai-massacre.html

Dr. Marsha Coleman-Adebayo Biography (2017) The NO FEAR Institute. https:// thenofearinstitute.wordpress.com/about/dr-marsha-coleman-adebayo-biography/

Elliston, Frederick, Keenan, John, Lockhart, Paula and van Schaik, Jane (1985) *Whistleblowing: Managing Dissent in the Workplace.* New York: Praeger Publishers.

Geng, Veronica (1973, April 29) Thalidomide: The American experience. *New York Times.* http://www.nytimes.com/1973/04/29/archives/thalidomide-the-american -experience.html

Goldstein, Matthew (2017, April 18) Harbert reaches $40 million tax settlement with New York. *New York Times.* https://www.nytimes.com/2017/04/18/business/ dealbook/harbert-management-harbinger-capital-falcone.html?rref=collection %2Ftimestopic%2FWhistle-Blowers&mtrref=undefined&gwh=D7593032B498 FB6D7B8CDF3E95EBD39F&gwt=pay

Johnson, Roberta. A. (2003) *Whistleblowing: When It Works and Why.* Boulder, CO: Lynne Rienner Publishers.

Kerr, Derek and Rivero, Maria (2014, April 30) Whistleblower Peter Buxtun and the Tuskegee Syphilis Study. *Government Accountability Project.* https://www .whistleblower.org/blog/04302014-whistleblower-peter-buxtun-and-tuskegee -syphilis-study

Kohn, Stephen. M. (2011, June 12) The whistle-blowers of 1777. *New York Times.* http://www.nytimes.com/2011/06/13/opinion/13kohn.html?mtrref=undefined&gwh =9038EA885097F19068B9FEDAC087325F&gwt=pay&assetType=opinion

Kross, Peter (2007, February 20) John Paul Vann: Man and legend. *History.net.* http:// www.historynet.com/john-paul-vann-man-and-legend.htm

Leung, Rebecca (2004, May 21) Gen. Zinni: "They've screwed up." *CBS 60 Minutes.* http://www.cbsnews.com/news/gen-zinni-theyve-screwed-up/

Malnick, Edward (2014, December 30) Margaret Thatcher warned officials not to be too harsh on Belgrano whistleblower. *Telegraph.* http://www.telegraph.co.uk/news/ politics/margaret-thatcher/11314284/Margaret-Thatcher-warned-officials-not-to-be -too-harsh-on-Belgrano-whistleblower.html

Maugh, Thomas H. III (2007, August 28) John Gofman, 88; physicist warned about radiation risks. *Los Angeles Times.* http://articles.latimes.com/2007/aug/28/local/me -gofman28

Miethe, Terance. D. (1999) *Whistleblowing at Work: Tough Choices in Exposing Fraud, Waste, and Abuse on the Job.* Boulder, CO: Westview Press.

Nader, Ralph, Petkas, Peter and Blackwell, Kate (1972) *Whistleblowing: The Report of the Conference on Professional Responsibility.* New York: Grossman Publishers.

O'Leary, Rosemary (2014) *The Ethics of Dissent: Managing Guerrilla Government.* Second edition. Thousand Oaks, CA: Sage.

Rabinowitz, Ted (2013, Fall) Frank Snepp '65, '68 SIPA chases the truth from Saigon to Los Angeles. *Columbia College Today.* https://www.college.columbia.edu/cct/ archive/fall13/alumni_profiles1

Rashke, Richard (2015, August 3) Blowing the whistle on educational inequity: Trudi Lytle. *Historic Heroines.* http://historicheroines.org/2015/08/03/blowing-the -whistle-on-educational-inequity-trudi-lytle/

Sanjour, William (1995, Summer) What's wrong with the EPA? *Greens.* http://www
.greens.org/s-r/078/07-48.html

Smith, John. L. Jr. (2013, December 19) Benjamin Franklin: America's first whistle-blower. *Journal of the American Revolution.* https://allthingsliberty.com/2013/12/
benjamin-franklin-americas-first-whistleblower/

Staff, Biography (2014, April 2) Daniel Ellsberg. *Biography.* https://www.biography
.com/people/daniel-ellsberg-17176398

Staff, CNN (1998, February 27) FBI whistle-blower leaves, gets $1.16 million. *CNN.*
http://www.cnn.com/US/9802/27/fbi.whitehurst/

Staff, CQ Almanac (1967) Automobile and highway safety programs implemented. *CQ
Almanac.* https://library.cqpress.com/cqalmanac/document.php?id=cqal67-1312984

Staff, Government Accountability Project (2017a) Bio: William Binney and J. Kirk
Wiebe. *Government Accountability Project.* https://www.whistleblower.org/node/
85

Staff, Government Accountability Project. (2017b). Franz Gayl, troop safety whistle-blower. *Government Accountability Project.* https://www.whistleblower.org/franz
-gayl-troop-safety-whistleblower

Staff, National Whistleblower Center (2017a) Coleen Rowley. *National Whistleblower
Center.* http://www.whistleblowers.org/index.php?option=com_content&task=view
&id=83

Staff, National Whistleblower Center (2017b). Julia Davis. *National Whistleblower
Center.* http://www.whistleblowers.org/index.php?option=com_content&task=view
&id=1181

Staff, National Whistleblower Center (2017c) Lieutenant Colonel Darrel
Vandeveld. *National Whistleblower Center.* http://www.whistleblowers.org/
meet-the-whistleblowers/1101-lieutenant-colonel-darrel-vandeveld

Staff, New York Times (1998, January 29) Unfair visa profiles. *New York Times.* http://
www.nytimes.com/1998/01/29/opinion/unfair-visa-profiles.html

Staff, theguardian (2001, November 25) Blowing the final whistle. *theguardian.* https://
www.theguardian.com/business/2001/nov/25/businessofresearch.research

Staff, The Whistleblower Directory. http://whistleblowerdirectory.com/whistleblowers
-v-z/

Staff, TIME (2005, August 28) Whistleblower SHAWN CARPENTER talks exclu-sively to TIME about the Chinese cyberespionage ring, Titan Rain. *TIME.* http://
content.time.com/time/press_releases/article/0,8599,1098911,00.html

Stein, Mark. A. (1992, March 31) Fired quality-control engineer alleges defective
subway work. *Los Angeles Times.* http://articles.latimes.com/1992-03-31/local/me
-271_1_quality-control-engineer

Tapper, Jake (2015, April 20) FBI agent testifies in Paula Broadwell cyberstalking case.
CNN. http://www.cnn.com/2015/04/19/politics/david-petraeus-paula-broadwell-fbi
-case/index.html

Taylor, Guy (2013, June 26) State Department has a dearth of diplomats to award for
dissent. *Washington Times.* http://www.washingtontimes.com/news/2013/jun/26/
state-department-has-a-dearth-of-diplomats-to-awar/

Von Drehle, David (2005, June 1) FBI's no. 2 was "deep throat": Mark Felt ends
30-year mystery of The Post's Watergate source. *Washington Post.* https://www
.washingtonpost.com/politics/fbis-no-2-was-deep-throat-mark-felt-ends-30-year
-mystery-of-the-posts-watergate-source/2012/06/04/gJQAwseRIV_story.html?utm
_term=.1853387fbf34

5. Businesslike government, but not as a business

THE BUSINESS MODEL

With the advent of industrialization in the nineteenth century, an increasingly complex economy required increasingly efficient governments at all levels. States and localities were called upon to provide essential services: highways and harbors, public health and hospitals, water and sewage systems, public schools and higher education, policing and firefighting, and many other functions. Citizens and corporations were expected to provide taxes to underwrite those investments in common purposes, and in return expectations as to efficient use of those resources were underscored. But incompetence characterized President Andrew Jackson's Spoils System through most of the nineteenth century. The Jacksonian assumption that anyone was capable of the so-called "simple" tasks of public management was no longer tolerable. Inefficiency, theft and illegal actions noticeably and intolerably interfered with the need for reliable, effective services.

In 1883 the US Pendleton Civil Service Act codified merit as the basis for many civil service appointments, and that principle now governs almost all government employees at all levels. States and cities followed the federal lead, and now more than 90 percent of public employees, at all levels of government, are required to have credentials and/or take competitive examinations.

Professor Woodrow Wilson, decades prior to becoming President, captured that progress, and the public's expectations, in his 1887 essay, "The study of administration." Drawing from the Good Government Movement, Wilson wrote:

> It is the object of administrative study to discover, first, what government can properly and successfully do and, secondly, how it can do these proper things with the utmost possible efficiency and at the least possible cost either of money or of energy ... The field of administration is a field of business ... Administrative questions are not political questions. Although politics sets the tasks for administration, it should not be suffered to manipulate its offices ... There should be a science of administration which shall seek to strengthen the paths of government, to make business less unbusinesslike, to strengthen and purify its organization, and to crown its dutifulness. (Woodrow Wilson, 1887)

Responding to Wilson's first objective, we have long established what government "properly and successfully" should accomplish. The scope of government's services is broad and impressive, delivering important services that individuals cannot achieve by themselves. All of these essential services contribute directly or indirectly to the efficacy of our economy and the quality of life of our citizens. All represent necessary and collective investments in our society, investments that we expect will be made efficiently, prudently and ethically. Nevertheless, few citizens comprehend the full scope of those initiatives. And many of us do not credit government with the progress in our standard of living that those systems make possible.

Wilson drew a bright line between policymaking and policy implementation. The former was a function of the political process; the latter was a function of professionalism, competence and a deep respect for policy. In 1900 Frank Goodnow explicitly offered that "politics has to do with the guiding or influencing of governmental policy, while administration has to do with the execution of that policy." In pursuit of Wilson's objective of scientific administration, and the complementary arguments of many scholars such as Goodnow, as well as citizens and interest groups, good governance stressed efficient service delivery in order to keep government's promises to its citizens. In New York City a leading good government group formed as the Bureau of City Betterment and incorporated in 1907 as the Bureau of Municipal Research (BMR), later becoming the Institute for Public Administration, dedicated to the proposition that "wasteful, ineffective government could not serve democracy well and could not provide the kind of services required by the new urban society" (Dahlberg, 1966). Schachter (2005) describes progressive initiatives that the BMR placed on the public agenda, for example:

> a report on public safety, the BMR (1913) argues that much police work is inefficient because no one knows the best methods of investigating crimes; to maximize efficient government, citizens as well as administrators must spend time collecting and analyzing data ... they should enforce requirements that records be kept ... they must instruct politicians and bureaucrats on what citizens want and remonstrate with them when they do not seem to respond.

In Boston, the Good Government Association of businessmen pursued progressive reforms in the first third of the twentieth century, including the management of budgets and contracts relating to municipal infrastructure projects in Boston; inspection of the city budget and the activities of the Finance Commission. According to Schachter (2002):

> Thirteen other urban research bureaus existed by 1914 ... bureaus in New York, Philadelphia and elsewhere had many of the same objectives – to prevent waste, to

find the best means of doing work in health, recreation and other substantive fields and to promote new activities for cities to undertake.

Hundreds of academic-practitioner societies, associations, councils and centers continue to contribute to government's capabilities in the US and globally. Among the most prominent in the US are the American Society for Public Administration (ASPA), the International City and County Management Association (ICMA), Association for Budgeting and Financial Management (ABFM), Association for Public Policy and Management (APPAM), Council of State Governments (CSG), Association of Government Accountants (AGA), National Association of State Budget Officers (NASBO) and National Center for Public Performance (NCPP). Together, they represent a compelling body of evidence as to government's competency, a refutation of the superficial assumption that government must be more businesslike.

Honest, competent government has become the ideal. The Good Government Movement established that the implementation of public priorities, or policies, should be delegated to impartial, neutral public managers. The underlying assumption was that public managers should not only be neutral and honest, but that they should be competent to carry out the responsibilities of their positions. Efficiency was key. Reformers repeatedly appealed for integrity and efficiency in government. Professional, efficient management was the expectation, and was condensed into the adage that "There is neither a Democratic nor a Republican way to build a road, just the right way."

In the early twentieth century, management experts and theorists, such as Frederick Taylor, Luther Gulick and Henri Fayol, were often called upon to make government "more businesslike." Taylor's "scientific management" model sought cooperation with the workforce via efficient methods, feedback on their performance, specialization of work, training workers in economies of time and energy, as well as separation of responsibilities between management and workers.

That model was to apply to government as well as to business, but it was often resisted in the public sector as too mechanistic, too industrial and too dehumanizing. Simple, comprehensive adages as to necessary competencies were developed to guide both sectors. A popular version was POSDCORB, attributed to Luther Gulick (Schachter, 2005):

- Planning – working out the things that the organization needs to get done
- Organizing – establishing formal structures of authority
- Staffing – establishing and maintaining the personnel function
- Directing – making decisions and leading
- Coordinating – relating the parts of the work
- Reporting – informing those to whom the executive is responsible

• Budgeting – planning fiscal matters, accounting and control

Other initiatives sought to build a rational, professional bureaucracy, but were criticized by Herbert Simon as a set of rigid "proverbs" which were often contradictory and untested. Simon argued that "the acquisition of knowledge about public administration ... should be based in facts empirically derived, measured and verified ... as the necessity of objectivity" (Riccucci, 2010).

The public bureaucracy did become increasingly professionalized, and engineers filled many public management position. In the 1920s the curricular foundation for public management as taught in the new schools of public administration included a broad curriculum based on values as well as skills, often from a political science perspective. Syracuse University established the Maxwell School of Citizenship and Public Affairs in 1924. Complementing an emphasis on citizenship, as the first professional degree in the field, it aspired to train practitioners in public affairs. The vision was to empower informed citizens who, immediately upon entering government careers, would effect change by professionalizing the public service. Thus, when the Maxwell School of Citizenship and Public Affairs opened on October 3, 1924, it included a citizenship curriculum for all undergraduates in the liberal arts, and its first cohort was six graduate students in the emerging field of public administration. In 1938 Harvard University announced the official opening of the Littauer Graduate School of Public Administration, now the Kennedy School of Government. In 1939 the American Society for Public Administration was founded to study the implementation of government policy dedicated to the science, processes and art of public administration. Today, at least 300 public administration programs in the US, and many more across the globe, offer degrees and certificates that equip public managers to manage competently – and to do so with much broader perspectives – sociology, psychology, economics, law – than were found in the century-old "scientific" curricula.

In terms of administrative practice, in 1937, under President Franklin Roosevelt, The President's Committee on Administrative Management, or the Brownlow Committee as it became known after its chair, Louis Brownlow, set forth a menu of extensive reforms in the federal government; similar bodies emulated that work at the state and local levels. World War II emphasized the need for efficiencies to drive enormous efforts toward victory. In the late 1940s the recommendations of the Hoover Commission on Organization of the Executive Branch of the Government added impetus to the assumption that government should be operated with businesslike efficiency. And it has.

At the federal, state and local levels governments have delivered services that are bargains:

- The average annual tuition and fees at ranked colleges in the US in 2021–22 was $38,185 at private colleges, as compared to $22,698 for out-of-state students at public colleges, and much less, $10,338 for in-state students at those public institutions (Kerr and Wood, 2022).
- According to the Center on Budget and Policy Priorities: "Medicaid provides more comprehensive benefits than private insurance at significantly lower out-of-pocket cost to beneficiaries; its lower payment rates to health care providers and lower administrative costs make the program very efficient. It costs Medicaid much less than private insurance to cover people of similar health status. For example, adults on Medicaid cost about 22 percent less than if they were covered by private insurance, Urban Institute research shows." (Coughlin et al., 2013)
- A US Postal Service (USPS) first-class letter costs 60 cents. United Parcel Service and Federal Express charge almost 20 times as much for comparable delivery timelines, and almost twice as much for a tracking service comparable to USPS Priority Mail.
- Overall, the public workforce is paid substantially less than their private sector counterparts for comparable work. In October 2020, the Federal Salary Council, surveying more than 250 occupations, pegged the public-private pay gap at 23 percent (Fehrer, 2020). That differentiation is even greater at the upper echelons of large private and public organizations. Cabinet Secretaries heading Federal departments with hundreds of thousands of employees are paid about $225,000; Corporate CEOs leading equally large endeavors earn millions, sometimes tens of millions, of dollars annually.

But despite all the progress in building efficiencies into the public sector, the myth has taken hold – indeed it has survived and gained momentum – that somehow government is inherently inefficient and that putting the business community directly in charge would solve that problem. Naive claims by candidates for elected office that government should be run like a business repeatedly draw on the same rhetoric, but without any acknowledgments that government is not a business, and with willful ignorance of government's capacities, achievements and continuous improvements. They simply recycle the phrase "Government should be run like a business," and have been doing so for well over a century.

That continuing argument runs counter to instances in which the private sector has proven unable to deliver affordable services, and the public sector had to step in to keep them up and running. Passenger rail became a money losing proposition for the railroads; they are now operated by Amtrak, a government corporation. Subway service, largely established as business ventures, are now completely operated by such government entities as the Metropolitan Transportation Authority, a state agency in New York. The Bear Mountain Bridge, an essential link over the Hudson River, was built by the Harriman Family as a toll bridge; it is now operated by New York State. Other amenities have become public "wards" of the state, such as private estates that have become parkland when their upkeep and taxes have become too expensive for their private owners. Mansions have become publicly owned museums.

Government services have been established to fill voids that societies can no longer address at the family or community, nonprofit and voluntary levels. Public hospitals often serve patients without private insurance or family support; private hospitals are often reluctant to do so and send those cases to their public counterparts. Public housing offers affordable shelter to those with constrained incomes while private landlords prefer to house low-income applicants only if they present vouchers from the government or if affordable housing is mandated as part of a builder's deal for approval of an upscale project.

Government spends enormous funds to invest in education, infrastructure, health, science, etc., but the returns or "profits" are not quantifiable on the government's books. Rather, they accrue to individuals and businesses – as intended. Those investments are more efficiently created as public goods and the government is expected to do so. Indeed, government was necessarily created thousands of years ago to facilitate commerce via roads and canals; to establish security against foreign invaders and domestic criminals; to protect the public's health in terms of plagues and transmissible illnesses; to deliver clean water; and scores of other functions.

The political, *ideologically* driven "business model" reemerged strongly under President Ronald Reagan in the 1980s. Early in his Administration he appointed the President's Private Sector Survey on Cost Control (the Grace Commission Private Sector Survey on Cost Control):

> I have just met with J. Peter Grace, who will be the new Chairman of the Private Sector Survey on Cost Control in the Federal Government. Mr. Grace is an outstanding businessman … and he promised me that he and his new team will work like tireless bloodhounds, leaving no stone unturned in their search to root out inefficiency and waste of taxpayer dollars. (Reagan, 1982)

Reagan went on to tout the Commission's work to his Cabinet and other appointees: "I'm determined that, when this administration leaves the stage, the American people will have a Federal Government that operates in a businesslike manner. Now, that means providing high-quality, essential public services as efficiently as possible. (Reagan, 1983)

Reagan viewed Grace and other businesspeople as the efficiency experts who would "fix" government spending, ferreting out unnecessary expenditures. Legions of corporate executives made quick trips to agencies in Washington, DC, generating almost 2,500 recommendations and exaggerated, off-the-cuff estimates as to waste and presumed savings; almost nothing resulted. Rather, the Grace Commission was pursuing the interests of the private sector in terms of outsourcing and shrinking what they viewed as "big government." Following Grace, Reagan appointed the President's Council on Integrity and Efficiency and the Cabinet Council on Management and Administration as continuing bodies to control costs and increase efficiency. They were equally unsuccessful.

Reagan appointed many corporate leaders – charismatic individuals who had practiced a straightforward form of top-down management – to his Cabinet, as have his Republican successors. Few were willing to acknowledge how difficult were the demanding jobs of leading a government agency. As Ludvig von Mises, the leading theorist of the Austrian School of the twentieth century, observed (von Mises, 2017):

> It is vain to advocate a bureaucratic reform through the appointment of businessmen as heads of various departments ... A former entrepreneur who is given charge of a government bureau is in this capacity no longer a businessman but a bureaucrat. His objective can no longer be profit, but compliance with the rules and regulations ... It is a widespread illusion that the efficiency of government bureaus could be improved by management engineers and their methods of scientific management ... Such plans stem from a radical misconstruction of the objectives of civil government.

THE MYTH OF PRIVATIZATION

President Reagan's antipathy toward government – famously terming it the problem, not the solution – helped rebrand the business model as "privatization." In 1992, Professor E.S. Savas, perhaps the most prominent academic proponent of privatization, held that "It's Time to Privatize" (Savas, 1992):

> The proven productivity strategy is privatization by competitive contracting for municipal services ... Government services are often costly and poor not because the people who work in government are inferior to those who work in the private sector; they are not. It is because monopoly is generally inferior to competition in providing high-quality, low-cost goods and services, and most government activities are unnecessarily organized and run as monopolies. Privatization, when properly carried out, gives public officials and the public a choice, which fosters competition and leads to more cost-effective performance.

From a narrow perspective, contracting out may or may not save modest
sums, and there is no question that government service must be delivered efficiently. Government should, of course, be businesslike, that is, professional.
But the private sector model is not a magic template for public management.
Privatization brings with it several inherent problems when applied to the
delivery of government's promised services:

*   In business, a good deal of that creativity is devoted to constructing barri-
    ers to transactions that are considered unprofitable or undesirable. Banks
    may not serve low-income neighborhoods. Stores may require credit cards
    rather than cash, excluding potential customers without credit. Charter
    schools may claim that they are not equipped to serve children with learn-
    ing or physical disabilities, leaving more expensive remedial services to
    the public schools. Private hospitals and clinics may offload their difficult
    cases to their public counterparts. Yet public services have been estab-
    lished to serve all citizens and must legally do so.
*   Businesses may be tempted to narrow their services as a means to increas-
    ing their profit margins. A narrow interpretation of prison services that
    have been contracted out to private corporations has resulted in decreases
    in the quality of food, health care education and of counseling. Residents of
    privatized public housing have suffered loss of heat, long-deferred mainte-
    nance projects and summary evictions. Tolls to traverse privatized roads or
    bridges have become much more expensive.
*   The private sector, no matter what it might promise, will always pay exec-
    utives salaries that are excessive by public sector standards, will "cream"
    clienteles that are considered unprofitable to serve, and will limit clients
    and services in order to minimize costs and increase profits.

No government service is more important that the supply of clean water, and
Public Citizen's Campaign to Keep Water as a Public Trust has compiled
"Top 10 Reasons to Oppose Water Privatization" (Box 5.1), a set of findings
that should alert public service providers to the consequences of privatization
across a broad range of service areas.

BOX 5.1   TOP 10 REASONS TO OPPOSE WATER
PRIVATIZATION

The World Bank has predicted that by 2025, two-thirds of the world's population will run short of fresh drinking water. Given such a grim outlook,
it comes as little surprise that Fortune magazine recently defined water as
"the oil of the 21st century." Poised to capitalize on this crisis are private

companies, many of which are multinationals whose tentacles are probing the planet for opportunities to turn the misery of water-starved regions into profits for their executives and stockholders.

Instead of protecting existing supplies, enhancing conservation efforts, helping vulnerable populations, curbing pollution and raising public awareness, more and more government officials throughout the world are turning to privatization — transferring the control of this precious resource from the public sector to the private sector.

It is no underestimation to say that the very survival of untold millions of people could rest on decisions being made today — largely behind closed doors — in corporate boardrooms and government offices throughout the world. With each drop of water that falls into the hands of private interests, any sustainable solution to the global water crisis moves further and further from the public's grasp.

Privatization Leads to Rate Increases

Corporations have utilized rate hikes to maximize profits, which, by definition, is their bottom line. This bottom line often comes at the expense of water quality and customer service, but not at the expense of maintaining inflated executive salaries. Among the more unseemly aspects of handling water as a marketable commodity, rather than a basic human need and a natural resource, is that the poor are often denied access. Because living without water is not an option, people are often forced to consume unsafe water, lest be faced with going without food, medicine or education.

Privatization Undermines Water Quality

Because corporate agendas are driven by profits rather than the public good, privatization usually results in the compromising of environmental standards. The National Association of Water Companies (NAWC), which represents the U.S. private water industry, intensively and perennially lobbies Congress and the Environmental Protection Agency to refrain from adopting higher water quality standards. The NAWC also persistently requests that all federal regulations be based on sound cost-benefit analysis, which means that public health is compromised for the sake of higher profits.

Companies Are Accountable to Shareholders, Not Consumers

In many cases, deals that government agencies make with water companies include exclusive distribution rights for 25 to 30 years, effectively sanctioning a monopoly. Companies are under little pressure to respond to customer concerns, especially when the product in question is not a luxury item that families can do without if they are dissatisfied with the performance of the only provider.

Privatization Fosters Corruption

The very structures of privatization encourage corruption. Checks and balances that could prevent corruption, such as accountability and transparency, are missing at every step of the process, from bidding on a contract to delivering water. Contracts are usually worked out behind closed doors with the details often still kept secret after the contract is signed, even though it is the public that will be directly affected by the conditions of the contract.

This situation opens itself up to bribery, which, if recent scandals throughout the world are any indication, is not an uncommon occurrence.

Privatization Reduces Local Control and Public Rights

When water services are privatized, very little can be done to ensure that the company – be it domestic, foreign or transnational – will work in the best interest of the community. Furthermore, if a community is dissatisfied with the performance of the company, buying back the water rights is a very difficult and costly proposition. Again, the prime directive of the water companies is to maximize profits, not protect consumers.

Private Financing Costs More than Public Financing

There is a false perception that when water services are privatized, the financial burden will shift from the public to the private sector, which will save taxpayer money by assuming the costs of repairing, upgrading and maintaining infrastructure. In reality, taxpayers simply wind up paying for these projects through their monthly bills. Tax-free public financing translates into lower-cost projects, while taxable private financing results in higher interest rates. As a result, consumers are also forced to make these higher payments on company loans.

Privatization Leads to Job Losses

Massive layoffs often follow in the wake of privatization, as companies try to minimize costs and increase profits. At times, service and water quality are put at risk due to understaffing. As a result, layoffs can be devastating not only to the workers and their families, but to consumers as well.

The very structures of privatization encourage corruption. Checks and balances that could prevent corruption, such as accountability and transparency, are missing at every step of the process, from bidding on a contract to delivering water. Contracts are usually worked out behind closed doors with the details often still kept secret after the contract is signed, even though it is the public that will be directly affected by the conditions of the contract.

This situation opens itself up to bribery, which, if recent scandals throughout the world are any indication, is not an uncommon occurrence.

Privatization Reduces Local Control and Public Rights

When water services are privatized, very little can be done to ensure that the company – be it domestic, foreign or transnational – will work in the best interest of the community. Furthermore, if a community is dissatisfied with the performance of the company, buying back the water rights is a very difficult and costly proposition. Again, the prime directive of the water companies is to maximize profits, not protect consumers.

Private Financing Costs More than Public Financing

There is a false perception that when water services are privatized, the financial burden will shift from the public to the private sector, which will save taxpayer money by assuming the costs of repairing, upgrading and maintaining infrastructure. In reality, taxpayers simply wind up paying for these projects through their monthly bills. Tax-free public financing translates into lower-cost projects, while taxable private financing results in higher interest rates. As a result, consumers are also forced to make these higher payments on company loans.

Privatization is Difficult to Reverse

Once a government agency hands over its water system to a private company, withdrawing from the agreement borders on the impossible. Proving breach of contract is a difficult and costly ordeal. And multinational trade agreements provide corporations with powerful legal recourse. A private company, for example, can use the North American Free Trade Agreement's secretive tribunals to contest challenges to privatization. And in World Bank loan deals, which often makes water privatization a condition, companies are usually guaranteed cash payments if a government agency returns its water system to public control.

Privatization Can Leave the Poor with No Access to Clean Water

Contrary to public assertions, World Bank and International Monetary Fund privatization schemes in the developing world usually result in reduced access to water for the poor. "Structural adjustment" programs foisted upon governments seeking loans often include water privatization as a condition. Impoverished, politically enfeebled countries are hardly in a position to refuse these conditions, as doing so would cause them to default on their debts. As a result, the World Bank and IMF are able to provide lucrative and virtually risk-free contracts for multinationals, due to guaranteed rates of return and investment protection clauses.

Privatization Would Open the Door for Bulk Water Exports

Fully aware of bleak water supply prognostications, corporations are in a mad dash to obtain access to fresh water that they can sell at huge profits, as high as 35 percent. It goes without saying that those who control water supplies will exercise economic and political power at almost unimaginable degrees. Bulk water exports – transporting water from water-rich countries to water-poor countries – could have disastrous consequences. Massive extraction of water from its natural sources can result in ecological imbalance and destruction. Disrupting aquifers by over-extraction often damages the environment and socioeconomic standards. Groundwater is being over-extracted as it is, and once aquifers are emptied or polluted, they are almost impossible to restore.

Source: Reprinted with permission from Public Citizen (n.d.).

It is, then, important for public sector decision-makers to understand that government and business differ on deep-seated assumptions. After nearly a century of the business model, in 1958 Wallace Sayre was compelled to conclude that business and government are distinctly different. Sayre held that: "public and private management are fundamentally alike in all unimportant respects." In a 1976 review article addressing the proposition that public and private organizations were converging in terms of important characteristics, the authors concluded that (Rainey, Backoff and Levine, 1976):

> optimal preparation for management in the two types of organizations would call for different emphases, some of which readily come to mind – more emphasis on political institutions and processes, on government budgeting, on public policy analysis, and on administrative law instead of business law … In sum, there are indications of

a number of important differences between public and private organizations, which cannot be ignored in considerations of management research, training, and practice.

Citing Sayre, in 1980, in an address to the Public Management Research Conference, Graham Allison enumerated more than two dozen differences between public and private organizations. His review of the literature posited that public organizations had (Allison, 1980):

- Greater diversity of intensity of external informal influences on decisions (bargaining, public opinion, interest group reactions)
- Greater need for support of constituencies – client groups, sympathetic formal authorities, etc.
- Broader impact, greater symbolic significance of actions of public administrators
- Wider scope of concern, such as public interest
- Greater public scrutiny of public officials and their actions
- Greater public expectations that public officials act with more fairness, responsiveness, accountability and honesty
- Greater multiplicity and diversity of objectives and criteria
- Greater tendency of goals to be conflicting (more tradeoffs).

Public administration scholars in the twenty-first century continue to reinforce Sayre's conclusion. Examining a representative range of important social services in 2003, David Van Slyke presented evidence of systemic privatization failures. Services were not delivered in a timely manner. Decisions were more political than economic. Fraud was common. Clients were abused. Expenditures for health care were avoided. Public schools lost resources. Per capita costs rose. Programs were "cherry picked" to avoid serving individuals who required costly services. Services were disrupted, etc. (Van Slyke, 2003).

Reinforcing Sayre, in 2012 John Harvey advised: "We should no more want the government to be run like a business than a business to be run like the government. The key issue is this: not everything that is profitable is of social value and not everything of social value is profitable. The proper role of government is the latter" (Harvey, 2012).

And in 2019, Jeffrey Mohler concluded that:

> And when it comes to saving money, the evidence is mixed at best. In many cases, privatization turns out to be far more costly. A 2007 survey found that over half of the local governments that placed services back under public control did so because privatization didn't cut costs. (Mohler, 2019)

Government agencies operate in a much more complex and political decision-making environment than their private counterparts. In the private sector, decisions are typically made by a few executives at the top of the hierarchy. In government, multiple constituencies are represented in the legislative branch where policy direction and oversight are paramount. Diversity and the perspectives that follow it are expected in the executive branch. Decisions are evaluated via judicial action within the framework of constitutions, laws and regulations. Unions have a voice in the policy implementation process. Interest groups make their preferences known on every issue.

Businesses operate in pursuit of profits or sales or market share. Public services have no such simple metrics, no one bottom line. Every public service is viewed by stakeholders through multiple lenses, and multiple measures do not add up to the neat and simple metrics – profit and loss, price of stocks, total sales – that drive markets. Government services cannot be easily reduced to a few simple measures. Each service may have multiple goals; each can be gauged by metrics that cover services, outputs, outcomes and impacts. Many results are not easily measurable as they accrue to individual citizens and businesses. Results may be very long term and indirect. Some results may be invisible, such as terrorist attacks, accidents or illnesses that are avoided as a function of government's efforts.

When agencies make seemingly arbitrary bureaucratic decisions, it is typically because they are adhering to the law and its derivative regulations; private corporations have much more discretion and degrees of freedom. That is, government is, to some extent, deliberately inefficient. The need for approvals and oversight is a purposeful drag to ensure compliance with the law and regulations, with ethics, and with procedures. The need to serve everyone is itself inherently inefficient as those clients may be people that businesses often avoid – students with learning disabilities who are turned away by private schools; services that are time consuming and not cost-effective such as selling a few stamps to someone at the post office. Costly services cannot be summarily dropped or consolidated, such as rural post offices or very small police departments, because they provide considerable public value in terms of serving or identifying small communities.

Ethical norms are emphasized more strongly in the public sector. Codes of Ethics encompass the breadth of such guidance, and public organizations are much more likely to hold their workforces to those standards. This is not to say that the private sector is inherently unethical, but simply that ethics is more apparent and "upfront" in training, practice and oversight across government organizations.

Democratic values are foundational principles for public organizations, whereas private companies are not held as extensively to that standard. Yes, many private companies have shareholder meetings, sometimes generating surprising outcomes, although most shareholders have no voice. But all government agencies are subject to the "will of the people" in terms of legislative actions, budgetary or otherwise. All public agencies are expected to answer to the public for their actions, inactions or grievous errors. And the media directs much more attention to critiques of government policies or procedures than they do to corporate parallels.

In contrast, privatization erodes public responsibility by minimizing input from stakeholders. As Avihay Dorfman and Alon Harel observe in "Against privatisation as such" (Dorfman and Harel, 2015):

> the typical arguments concerning privatisation are instrumental, relying heavily on comparing the performance of a public functionary with that of its private counterpart. This article challenges this approach for leaving unaddressed other important consequences of shifting responsibilities to private entities ... privatisation cuts off the link between processes of decision-making and the citizens, and therefore erodes political engagement and its underlying notion of shared responsibility. It is also the transformation of our political system to ones characterised by fragmentation and sectarianism.

Chiara Cordelli enhances the contrast between considerations of efficient instrumentality, or the dominant argument for privatization, and considerations of political legitimacy, or grave reservations about the erosion of our political values. Cordelli asks:

> Can justice ever be achieved, and can democratic legitimacy ever be secured, in a privatized state? What ethical considerations should guide debates about the expanding privatization of government? When is the use of private means for public ends morally objectionable, and why? Are there public functions that should never be delegated to private actors, even if by outsourcing them a government could achieve better results?

She warns of: "the increasing dispersion of political power at the domestic level, through systematic processes of privatization and outsourcing" (Cordelli, 2020).

Most recently, Donald Cohen and Allen Mikaelian published a comprehensive critique, *The Privatization of Everything: How the Plunder of Public Goods Transformed America and How We Can Fight Back* (Cohen and Mikaelian, 2021). Drawing on a large body of evidence that privatization of public goods degrades our public, democratic values, they outlined "Six Steps to Regaining Public Control over Public Goods":

(1)   The supposed private-sector efficiency that's often promised to bring savings typically disappears in inflated executive salaries and "administrative costs," and the profit motive proves irresistible.

(2)   Privatization is, in part, designed to close the door on public alternatives and programs and to eliminate public "competition" with the private sector.
(3)   Public decisions about public goods must remain fully in public hands; public decisions should strengthen and expand access to essential public goods – not weaken and exclude.

GOVERNMENT VS. GOVERNMENT: A PUBLIC COMPETITION MODEL

Savas was right about the advantages of competition. It does foster innovation and creativity. It does accelerate organizational learning and the search for good ideas. It does encourage creative problem solving.

But Savas and other proponents of privatization, such as the many candidates for elective office who tout that model, ignore the ill fit between business and government. They argue for the advantages of competition while ignoring the conflict with government values as enumerated above. In contrast, students of public administration understand that public services are not meant to turn a profit, or even to break even. Returns on public investments accrue elsewhere to individuals as an enhanced quality of life, and to businesses in a stronger bottom line.

Competition can lower costs, allow economies of scale, avoid large startup costs, provide access to specialized skills and training, etc. Increased competition results when bids or proposals for the delivery of a service are solicited from a range of producers. Competition is a good idea. But competition does have to mean privatization at the cost of public values and constrained services. We can achieve the advantages of competition without giving away control over services which really should be in the public domain. We should not want private sector firms running our prisons, certainly not our emergency response departments, and probably not our highways, bridges, water systems, and dozens of other services. What we really need to do is create more competitive entities in the public sector.

Government *can* develop a government-only model with the advantages of competition, at the same time incorporating the values and checks that are necessary in a responsive, ethical society. A government vs. government model, open only to competing public and associated nonprofit organizations, would exemplify the values of public service and would meet ethical expectations of honesty, fairness and the provision of services to all citizens. It could deliver public services, as promised, efficiently and effectively, under full public control. And it would markedly increase trust in government and in the public sector's use of the public's tax dollars.

"Govt. vs. Govt." would operate within the context of the values, commitments and ideals of public service. As a public sector alternative to the business model, to privatization and contracting out, it would create new public organizations, or offices in traditional organizations, competing with each other and with established government agencies, to deliver any of a broad array of services. Such startups would operate much as a conglomerate does, broadening the scope of their service offerings beyond traditional and confining service silos. It would induce innovation, efficiency and a greater focus on promised services and client satisfaction; the appointment of innovations officers would facilitate a search for best practices – technological, managerial, organizational, and along other dimensions of human interaction. Healthy competition to deliver public services could draw on thousands and thousands of extant public organizations and new entities whose missions would be simply to deliver essential services to the public efficiently and effectively, to achieve promised outcomes within the context of promised values, and to maintain public control of public resources under public oversight.

A public competition model could harness the creative problem-solving energies of a motivated public workforce. Generic Agencies (or offices) A, B, C etc. would effectively compete – all the while maintaining government's commitments to serve everyone and to do so fairly, openly and ethically. Multiple agencies would be established to bid on virtually any service areas. but only against other such government agencies. Private sector bidders would not be eligible.

CAPACITIES FOR COMPETITION

The public sector is primed to experiment with a government-only competitive mode, and the evidence underpinning that readiness is extensive. Shared services' organizational arrangements, already in place, are evidence of an emerging willingness to "shop around" for more efficient service delivery contracts, but totally within an umbrella of public sector expectations. Such arrangements, beyond privatization, are widespread, for instance, at the municipal level (Holzer and Fry, 2011):

•   Shared services, in which municipalities consolidate services, while retaining their identities and independence. Shared services are pursued to avoid redundancies and to make the best use of costly labor and equipment. Municipalities that cooperate to improve economies of scale can, therefore, operate to reduce costs per capita. One mechanism is through resources that are allocated in the budget that are not fully utilized or not utilized at their highest value in the pre-consolidated departments. This is not usually the result of poor planning. To the contrary, it is necessary to have resources beyond what is necessary for non-peak service needs so the municipality can respond to peaks or unforeseen service demands. A cooperative agreement is more efficient when it reduces the proportion of total resources that must be available for peak demand.

When towns cooperate to deliver a service, they broaden the service area beyond that which was served by either of the original departments, individually. If the cost stays the same but the population served increases, it reduces the cost per capita. In practical scenarios, for the department taking over the cooperative service delivery, the cost will increase, but not proportionately as much as the service increases. Like any delivery option, which benefits from economies of scale, there must be the potential for excess capacity in the pre-consolidated department due to the allocation of resources serving the original area, which can be used to advantage in a larger service area. The causes of the excess capacity may include equipment without adequate demand for full utilization, personnel with specialized skills without adequate demand to use those skills on a full-time basis, or staffing to meet peaks in service needs leading to the excess capacity during non-peak periods.

A service which a municipality can schedule provides a good opportunity for sharing expensive equipment and spreading the costs over a larger population. Because the service is scheduled, conflicts arising from needing to use the equipment at the same time can be avoided. Alternatively, if personnel are not fully utilized by the one municipality, sharing those personnel may provide full use and, therefore, more total service for the same cost. This works well for specialized personnel, who, for example, have the training to operate complex equipment, but when that equipment is not in use, perform tasks other, less highly compensated, employees can perform. Using the specialist skills as fully as possible increases efficiency.

An example of such an arrangement is the use of trained personnel and equipment for tree removal in neighboring towns. By contracting for the employees and equipment to remove and trim trees, a smaller municipality does not need to incur the cost of owning the equipment used or to pay higher wage rates for the more skilled employee even when they are performing other tasks requiring less skill.

• Joint municipal services that maintain responsibility and capability for service delivery. Joint services involve resources (such as personnel) from all the participants acting together as the service producer. The department head may be appointed jointly by each of the participants and may have the authority to schedule the employees and equipment to be used in the different municipalities as needed. It is advantageous for maintaining control and community identity.

- Special districts that create an additional entity; a special district is controlled by a governing body appointed by the recipient municipality or elected by the voters, often in a special election. It operates independently of the municipality, controlling its own budget and with its own administrative staff, duplicating the support functions of the municipality for the other services it delivers. It can be a regional district with multiple participants, which offsets the redundancy of administration.
- Management entities that address issues of control while achieving economies of scale. There are many variants of delivery alternatives that focus on managing the production of a service or services. These include councils of governments, joint meetings and joint boards. Their definition can vary from state to state and country to country, but they are focused on controlling the management of the production of the service or services for multiple recipients. They are sometimes a hybrid form in which the management entity is separate from the actual production organization, which also serves multiple recipients. The management entity provides better representation of the interests of all the participating municipalities.
- Production entities that emphasize efficiency in the production of services, taking responsibility from other municipalities. Other variants are focused on the operational aspects of the production process and may include the provision and management of the service. Examples include centralization to a regional or county producer; the agency model in which a larger level of government produces the service to fit the provision decisions of the participating municipalities individually, but with some control over those decisions exercised by the central body; and virtual governments, in which the municipality is a policymaking body only, leaving responsibility for production of all services to an administrative service center.

Other service delivery mechanisms which do not neatly fit in the above categories are franchising, co-production, and even the decision not to provide the service (solid waste is a good example in some areas). Each one is an attempt to find the best solution to the service needs as perceived at some point in time, weighing the advantages and disadvantages against other alternatives.

- Partnership governance, which refers to co-production, public-public, but also public-private partnerships (PPPs) in which the private sector partner adheres to the values of the public sector co-producer. PPPs have been defined by Seth Grossman (Grossman, 2015):

> Public-private partnerships are formed by and require multi-sectoral collaboration, both the process of arriving at consensus-oriented agreements as a mutual qualitative imperative, and the management, or implementation of the partnership, which requires collaboration, integrated multisectoral skills, and

management. These collaborations establish new publicly oriented organizations that enhance governance and public management ... The technologies of stronger long-term contracts, improved performance measurement, focused rewards, and new institutional arrangements all combine to promise superior productivity and performance in delivering public infrastructure.

The public and private realms have taken on more interdependent relationships in the twenty-first century. The rise of partnership governance describes the process of multi-sectoral engagement and can be appropriately associated with the evolution of democracy as a form of citizen action as well as the corresponding public management capacity. The blending and trading of private to public, and equally public to private technologies, is uniquely democratic, as is information and innovation as the foundation of modern economies. The need to partner across public and sectoral fields is emerging as a professional field of management, but one that often lacks performance data that can enhance the understanding of both public and private attributes involved in these partnerships. Partnership management and planning are skills well suited to the public manager. As we move toward a variety of partnership governance forms to solve social and technical problems, the field of public administration must identify and provide a variety of partnership management skills and the attributes of partnership governance.

Any such arrangements should, of course, be subject to agreements that provide for:

- Specification of the service with measurable indicators of quantity and quality
- Addressing fairness considerations
- Adapting to changing conditions
- Oversight, monitoring and follow-up modification mechanisms
- Mechanisms for the determination of cost and revenue sharing
- Opt-out and early termination clauses
- Documentation of the shared services innovation.

Governments identify opportunities for shared services by identifying better performing districts through benchmarking, award-winning best practices and analysis of services with cost or quality shortcomings. Those efforts often result in municipal services being delivered at a lower per capita cost and with improved outcomes if a shared service approach is followed (Table 5.1):

Table 5.1   *Municipal shared service options (typical opportunities)*

Service Types	Service Function	Service Types	Service Function
Public Works	Trash collection	Police	Investigation
Public Works	Roads – maintenance, sweeping	Police	Laboratory analysis
Public Works	Snow removal	Police	Traffic control
Public Works	Leaf removal	Police	Records
Public Works	Buildings maintenance	Police	Local ordinances
Public Works	Parks – grounds maintenance	Police	Patrol
Public Works	Storm water and pollution control systems maintenance	Police	Call response
Public Works	Waste water systems maintenance	Police	Communications (equipment)
Public Works	Water distribution systems maintenance	Fire	Prevention
Public Works	Forestry	Fire	Response
Public Works	Engineering	Fire	Investigation
Public Works	Infrastructure replacement and development	Fire	Inspections, regulations, records
Tax Collection	Payments, customer service, records	Fire	Equipment maintenance
Tax Collection	Liens and bankruptcies	Public Health	Clinics, immunization
Tax Assessment	Field work	Public Health	Residential inspection – infestations
Tax Assessment	Records, customer service	Public Health	Commercial Inspection
Finance	Accounting, records	Public Health	Environmental and sanitation
Finance	Purchasing, A/P	Public Health	Animal control
Court	Traffic records, pay, inquiries, trial	Public Health	Animal shelter
Court	Criminal warrants, trial	Cultural/ Recreation	Children's programs
Court	Municipal Fines – pay, Inquiries, trial	Cultural/ Recreation	Adult programs
Court	Neighbor disputes	Cultural/ Recreation	Senior programs
Court	Records and other administration	Management	General

Service Types	Service Function	Service Types	Service Function
Licensing, certifications	Dogs, Vital Statistics, mercantile	Management	Human resources
Municipal records (clerk)	Minutes, Agendas, Ordinances, Resolutions	Management	Grants, insurance
Municipal records (clerk)	Archiving and retrieval	Technology	Network, phones
Municipal Information	General and reception	Technology	Public (web, e-commerce)
Construction	Permitting and records	Planning	Code enforcement
Construction	Inspection	Planning	Land use
Dispatch		Planning	Development
EMS	Response	Planning	Zoning
Transportation	Parking, buses, airports		

PARTNERING BEYOND SILOS

Public organizations that necessarily provide services beyond their narrowly stated silos, or missions, have provided evidence of capacities to deliver services across a range of functional areas.

Public school systems are primarily focused on classroom-based learning. Empowering students to learn, however, requires a broad array of services. Transportation to school via school buses or public transit is often the first prerequisite, as is parking for faculty and staff. Once at school, students may require counseling, speech-language therapy, security, school-based health services, breakfast and lunch, social work and psychological counseling, adaptive physical education for accommodations in gym class, modifications to buildings for equal access, libraries and online access to databases, media systems, etc.

Large public universities, which are essentially small cities, incorporate all of the services that characterize school districts, and typically add: residence halls, health centers, athletic facilities ranging from fitness centers to large stadiums, extensive food services, career centers, campus police departments, theatres and professional theatre departments, study abroad programs, assistance with visa applications, media broadcasts, publishing and press operations, writing centers, support for gender, religious and national identity issues, etc.

Military bases are small cities as well, mirroring all of the services required by schools and universities, with a broader array of responsibilities for service members and their families. Many operate day care centers and K-12 schools, and also extend higher education opportunities on-site in cooperation with community colleges and universities. Housing, health care and security systems are extensive.

Prisons, national parks and airports are examples of other extensive public assets that deliver a range of services parallel to those noted above as municipal shared service options. Departments that provide policing, firefighting, recreation, senior services, museum and cultural programs and dozens of other local, regional, state and federal programs in the US have all developed areas of expertise that other agencies need not reinvent.

All of the public organizations noted above, and others as well, are capable of putting their expertise to work on a shared service basis across mission-specific silos and might well respond if opportunities to "showcase their wares" were available.

BUILDING COMPETENCIES FOR PUBLIC MANAGEMENT OF PUBLIC PROGRAMS

To support the provision of public services, the "science" of public administration was intended to foster the competencies of public managers. POSDCORB and other rules of thumb derived from the business model, however, were insufficient for the management of an increasingly complex public sector.

Over the last century the field of public administration, to its credit, has responded to the needs of public managers with hundreds of academic programs, offering a strong Master of Public Administration (MPA) curricula accredited by the National Association of Schools of Public Affairs and Administration, now the Network of Schools of Public Affairs and Administration. Master of Public Policy (MPP) programs have complemented the field in the last several decades. Together, MPA and MPP programs in the US graduate more than 10,000 public sector leaders annually.

That supply of graduates, however, falls substantially short of the need. The public sector at all levels employs something over 20 million public servants, including schools and the military; nonprofits that deliver government-related programs employ at least ten million more, for a total well in excess of 30 million. Several million of those are in supervisory, management and policy-level positions, of whom it is likely that far less than 10 percent, perhaps less than 5 percent, have MPA, MPP or even MBA degrees. Given the complex decision-making environment in the public sphere, this suggests a series of "supply chain" shortcomings that must be addressed.

UNDERGRADUATE PUBLIC SERVICE

First, undergraduate public service majors and minors must become much more widespread, often as a pathway to the MPA and MPP. As a sampler of

the knowledge and motivation that are foundational elements of public administration, they can highlight public service as a socially important option *and*
well-paying careers for students who are narrowly fixated on pursuing law,
business, medicine, science and other popular topics as majors.

Why create an undergraduate major in public and nonprofit service? The
goal of this major would be to highlight longstanding commitments to public
service. By presenting practical examples of public service in action, the major
would meet a student need by presenting career opportunities many students
may be unaware of, but well suited to, based upon personal commitments to
civic engagement and the common good.

The major would deepen an understanding of the spirit of civic engagement
already evident among many high school students who fulfill community
service degree requirements, and undergraduates who are committed to pursuing post-graduate experiences and career pathways to public service roles
in government, nonprofit and voluntary organizations, foundations, the media
and as citizen participants in the democratic process.

The major in public service would be grounded in our society's compelling
commitments to civic engagement and citizen service, embodying the ethical
principles of the common good, service to others and social equity. In recent
decades, leaders have advocated for civic engagement (Holzer, 2018):

> Senator Elizabeth Warren called for citizens "to get more directly involved in the
> democracy of policy ... Advocacy – getting involved in issues you care about and
> fighting for them – can reshape our country, and I guarantee it will reshape you."

Former Supreme Court Justice Sandra Day O'Connor spoke directly to students' career paths:

> I was having a better time at my job than were those of my peers who had opted
> for private practice. Life as a public servant was more interesting. The work was
> more challenging. The encouragement and guidance from good mentors was more
> genuine. And the opportunities to take initiative and to see real results were more
> frequent.

Three decades later President William Jefferson Clinton held that:

> Citizen service is the very American idea that we meet our challenges not as isolated
> individuals but as members of a true community, with all of us working together.
> Our mission is nothing less than to spark a renewed sense of obligation, a new sense
> of duty, a new season of service.

And in the twenty-first century President Barack Obama eloquently argued
that: "Our greatness as a nation has depended on our sense of mutual regard

for each other, of mutual responsibility. The idea that everybody has a stake in the country, that we're all in it together."

Beyond the call to serve, arguments and evidence of renewed calls for public service continue to be part of the policy dialogue. For example, the Federal Commission on Military, National and Public Service issued a major set of recommendations in January 2020, defining service as "a personal commitment of time, energy, and talent to a mission that contributes to the public good by protecting the national and its citizens, strengthening communities, or promoting the general social welfare." One of the Commission's highlighted alternatives "could be that all Americans fulfill a requirement of 600 hours of service before the age of 30." A major recommendation was to "Explore models in higher education that seek to raise the profile and attractiveness of public service and prepare outstanding high school graduates for careers in public service" (Federal Commission on Military, National and Public Service, 2020).

Public sector workforce demands combined with a supply of young people determined to make societal impact through their careers create a landscape suited to undergraduate public service education. However, such academic programs are uncommon.

There is great potential for attracting undergraduates to the study of public service. Young people are motivated by public sector values such as integrity, social equity, accountability, transparency, leadership and the public good. Millennials and Gen Z are engaged citizens committed to living out public service values through their careers. enroll tens of thousands of people who feel a calling to serve. However, government is not capitalizing upon its natural alignment with these values. Students typically express relatively high levels of interest in government employment at all levels, and nonprofit positions as well, but upon graduation from college or AmeriCorps and the Peace Corps default to private sector employment.

A model Bachelor of Science in Public Service (BSPS) major, outlined below, would expose students to career paths aligned with the values of democracy and public service in government, nonprofit organizations, public-private partnerships, voluntary organizations, foundations, political organizations and the media.

The BSPS is an interdisciplinary degree that cultivates a public service ethic, providing students with the understanding and experience of working in a public service domain with an emphasis on providing communities with "solutions" to wicked problems. Students will be prepared to help communities develop the competencies, systems and resources necessary for economic and social development.

Students would have the option of choosing one of two tracks: Concentration in Public Service Administration, or Concentration in Nonprofit Management.

The degree fosters hands-on, experiential learning, grounded in strong theoretical and scholarly academics. Students engage with faculty through courses, internships, research opportunities and community engagement.

The curriculum is interdisciplinary and emphasizes experiential learning, leadership, community collaboration and global reach. Courses are contemporary and relevant, reflecting the current and future needs of public service professions, and emphasize core competencies in specific areas (Box 5.2). The BSPS introduces students to organizations and practices that help to improve and advance the problem-solving capacities of public service organizations, or related organizations with public service orientations. The program provides students with an understanding of the breadth and depth of public service professions, while building their perspectives and capacities relative to delivering services to the public, as promised in our society's foundational documents. Students gain analytical skills through research and experiential learning opportunities, and analyze policies that have a direct impact on individuals, communities and organizations. The BSPS builds competencies – student knowledge, skills and abilities – to innovate in, respond to and adapt to the need for creative solutions to "wicked" problems in dynamic environments.

The degree is career-oriented, introducing students to a surprisingly wide range of opportunities in community, local, state and global institutions. Public, nonprofit and private and employment options are widespread, and represent approximately 40 percent of the workforce. Graduates are prepared to work in such professional positions as managers, researchers, analysts, advocates and community engagement specialists at competitive salaries. The BSPS can be pursued as part of a five-year program leading to the Master of Public Administration (MPA) degree, or related degrees such as the Master of Public Policy (MPP) The BSPS will, of course, prepare students to pursue the MPA or MPP at the hundreds of such programs nationally. Students will also be prepared to secure interim post-graduate opportunities in public service organizations such as the Peace Corps and AmeriCorps; they will then be well positioned to pursue the MPA, MPP or other graduate degrees upon completion of those service experiences.

BOX 5.2   UNDERGRADUATE PUBLIC SERVICE CURRICULUM. CORE COURSES

Public Service as Responsible Citizenship (3 cr)

Public Service as Responsible Citizenship is about people living together in democratic communities and the particular role community service plays in support of those communities. Community service in a wide variety of settings has become a significant way in which we accomplish public goals. This course critically examines the community service approach to "public work" and seeks to understand how service might be more effective in improving community life. Students will learn basic strategies and tactics utilized by individuals, groups and organizations to maintain and improve the quality of life in their communities.

Introduction to Public Administration (3 cr)

This introductory course is set within the context of contemporary, political, social and economic realities. It examines the policies and processes of governmental, nonprofit, health and institution-based programs from a multidisciplinary perspective. Students are introduced to the field and profession of public administration. Topics for discussion include the role of managers in publicly controlled bureaucracies, techniques for analyzing and participating in public policymaking including decision making, policy formulation, strategic planning, and implementation. Students also develop a broad understanding of the public sector while learning to think and act as an ethical public administration professional.

Introduction to Nonprofit Administration (3 cr)

This course focuses on government and nonprofit organizations in the delivery of human services. This course will benefit students who are interested in the role of government and nonprofit organizations in citizen engagement, delivery of public services, and the interconnectedness of government and nonprofit sector. This introductory course will provide students with an understanding of the breadth and depth of the public and nonprofit sectors from an economic and social impact perspective. Specific emphasis will be placed on nonprofit corporations, including coursework that explores the legal, structural and operational issues that are particular to specific services.

Ethical Public Service (3 cr)

This course examines selected ethical problems and dilemmas facing public servants, including conflict of interest, confidentiality, deception, the appearance of impropriety, official disobedience, whistleblowing, human rights, and the moral responsibilities of leaders and citizens.

Leadership for the Service Professions (3 cr)

Leadership for the Service Professions builds upon the skills and knowledge successful college graduates learn through their many years as students, including: collaboration, leadership, active citizenship, multicultural understanding, reflective thinking, critical analysis, and the ability to be a change agent in their community. Effective leadership is essential at any and all levels to ensure that the potential for social change and positive resolution inherent in conflict is realized. This course provides students with an understanding of public service leadership skills and traits that will be necessary to master in order to be effective public and nonprofit service administrators.

Technology and Public Service (3 cr)

Government and private organizations are recognizing the benefits of data-driven decision making. As such, all business and strategic operations of this era are deploying technologies to improve data integrity in order to better serve its constituency. The course introduces various technologies public organizations may use to collect, manage and disseminate information used to inform and administer public services.

The Arts and Culture of Public Service (3 cr)

The Arts and Culture of Public Service focuses on the connection between arts and cultural program and community building, based on the perspective that arts and cultural programs can be a vehicle of community change and enhancement. This course will examine the role that arts and cultural programs played in community development and consider that arts and cultural programs are a vital part of our public service commitment.

Democratic Foundations of Public Service (3 cr)

A survey of the foundational documents of public service in the American and international contexts, exploring the democratic processes and quality-of-life promises that have been communicated to citizens via political platforms, addresses, declarations, constitutions, charters, legislation, regulations, and other enduring messages.

Career Explorations in Public Service (1 cr)

Career Explorations in Public Service helps students develop a strong foundation for career decision planning through career inventories, research on careers and personal reflection. The course provides opportunities and resources for students to seek career information related to academic and occupational interests which form the foundation for sound career decision making. Students will receive career management skills to effectively identify, compete and secure professional career opportunities. Students are guided through individual and group exercises that assist in identifying needs, values, wants, interest and abilities. Students also learn job search, networking and interview skills in preparation for an internship or career search.

Service-learning Internship (4 cr)

Service-learning Internship I is designed to provide students with field experiences with community agencies to link academic work with meaningful community service that will benefit both the agency and the student. Agencies will benefit with the infusion of enthusiastic students to assist in the delivery of services to their clients and students will develop a deeper understanding of their role as leaders in their communities as well as increase their civic and citizenship skills. The director of the undergraduate major will work in conjunction with the Career Development Center and other campus units to place students in a viable internship.

Note: Course descriptions above are based upon the author's curriculum initiatives while a faculty member at the Rutgers University School of Public Affairs and Administration and the Suffolk University Institute of Public Service.

COMPETENCIES FOR ALL PUBLIC ADMINISTRATORS/MANAGERS

Second, a largely unaddressed concern is that those who do fill administrative and management positions may not have the full knowledge base that would enable high performance, that would avoid costly problems, that would help them deliver on government's promises. Engineers, doctors, scientists, educators, artists, writers, athletes and many professionals who are necessarily appointed to administrative positions are unlikely to have any formal education or training in administration or management, especially *public* management. Too many public sector programs and agencies are led by professionals with impressive licenses, certifications or degrees, but not with the formal knowledge required to direct public organizations.

There are surprisingly wide gaps in expectations for efficient and effective provision of public services, on the one hand, and inadequate preparation to lead such efforts, on the other. MPA graduates may have most, but not all, of that toolkit, depending on the competencies that their particular masters program has chosen to emphasize. Curriculum components for MPA programs typically cover some two dozen subject matter areas (Box 5.3), complemented by specializations or concentrations. Finance and Budgeting courses are ubiquitous (100 percent), closely followed by Quantitative Decision Methodology. But courses devoted to the applications of analytical and administrative tools to the solution of public problems have declined over the last several decades. This suggests that more space in the curriculum should be devoted to how to deliver knowledge via the application of analytical tools, knowledge that would help solve real-world public problems, thereby empowering graduates to act competently to manage public disputes and conflict resolution. Similarly, more courses should address applications of information systems and management to the public sector, such as e-government, database management, web technologies and geographic information systems (Holzer and Lin, 2007) (Box 5.3). An analysis of 118 individual competencies important to local government managers vis-à-vis the content of curricula of MPA programs with a concentration in local government found good coverage of competencies associated with administration, legal/institutional systems and technical/analytical skills, but less coverage of competencies associated with ethics, interpersonal communications, human relations, leadership, group processes and community building (Lazenby, 2010).

BOX 5.3   CURRICULUM COMPONENTS FOR MPA PROGRAMS

Political-Social-Economic Context of Public Administration – Knowledge of:

- cultural and social mores and patterns;
- political values and processes;
- governmental institutions, powers and relationships;
- economic systems, incentives and controls; and
- environmental factors and resource availabilities.

Analytical Tools-Quantitative and Non-Quantitative – Knowledge of:

- quantitative decision methodology, e.g., research design, accounting parametric and nonparametric statistics, linear programming, modeling;
- electronic data processing and information systems;
- e-government, database management, web technologies and geographic information systems;
- systems and procedures analysis, and behavioral science methodology, e.g., research design, organization surveys, work measurement;
- legal processes and controls.

Individual-Group-Organization Dynamics – Knowledge of:

- individual and group behavior, e.g., individual motivation, group motivation, dynamics of groups, modes of leadership;
- organization structure, process and dynamics, e.g., models, authority, development, strategies, decision making;
- communications theory and process and;
- professionalism and public service, e.g., evolution of public services, roles and standards of professions, characteristics of bureaucracies.

Policy Analysis – Knowledge of:

- application of analytical and administrative tools to solution of public problems;
- processes by which policy is formulated, implemented and evaluated.

Administrative and Management Processes – Knowledge of:

- administrative planning and organizational design;
- management systems and processes including leadership, decision making, direction, and organization development and change;
- personnel administration including staffing, training, and collective bargaining;
- finance and budgeting; program evaluation and control;
- performance measurement, management and improvement.

Even MPA graduates who have completed this curriculum typically do not, over the course of their careers, consult the academic research and related journal articles that would help them maintain or expand the skill sets they have acquired, and most of those journals are not salient to practitioners. Graduates of MPP programs are often at a loss as to how to implement promising policy initiatives, a significant "donut hole" in a policy-oriented curriculum. Perhaps a fifth of MBAs work in government, nonprofits and universities, but may be ill prepared for public-facing positions that require consultation, communication and the larger political context. Yet they may serve in more complex environments than their fellow MBAs typically encounter (Cherry and Dave, 1997). They may have highly respected degrees, but little or no training for the organizational and human resource complexities that they will encounter in government leadership.

Top-level managers, new to government or promoted into management, often acknowledge that frustration. Their agency's default is often experiential "on-the-job training," but almost never the comprehensive training they need from day one. The dominant assumption is that "on-the-job" training will suffice for anyone entering a public position. Few people, however, can manage a government intuitively.

Of course, governments do offer training programs. But the efficacy of that training is limited:

- Policy-level appointees may serve only a few years at or near the top of a department, agency, bureau or commission. In a rush to install new initiatives during their likely time in office, availing themselves of classes or workshops becomes a low priority, or no priority at all.
- In some jurisdictions, often local, part-time elected officials supervise line departments. They are unlikely to voluntarily enroll in administrative or supervisory classes.

- Training budgets are often considered low priorities in a budget process that is increasingly underfunded.
- Some training may be mandated, such as ethics or diversity. But most other topics, such as measuring and improving performance, are not.

To maintain, indeed to increase, the public's trust in the management of their tax dollars and the delivery of services, public sector agencies must require *all* public administrators and managers to acquire familiarity with the full toolkit of acknowledged competencies. They must also require refreshment of that knowledge on a regular basis, as is often required of doctors, lawyers, architects or other licensed or certified professionals. Academic programs must revise or supplement their curricula to incorporate the full menu of competencies. That knowledge base could be delivered across multiple formats: in person, as discrete modules via self-paced learning, and as apps on computers, tablets and phones.

There is a broad consensus on an array of necessary public management competencies. Some certificate programs, such as the Certified Public Manager (CPM) program in the US, are based on the assumption that executive jobs are complex and differ from the private sector in many important respects. As a "mini-MPA," CPM and other certificates offer participants a solid framework on public management theory.

CPM fosters and encourages the highest possible levels of competence and ethical practice by managers in state and other levels of government through a national body of professionally trained and oriented Certified Public Managers. Established in 1976 and encompassing 33 accredited members (30 states, the Metropolitan Washington Council of Governments, the District of Columbia and the U.S. Graduate School). CPM citation, the Certified Public Manager (CPM) Program's primary goal is to improve the performance of public sector managers and the organizational performance of state, local and federal governments.

CPM offers a "comprehensive course of study by which public managers can acquire and apply the best practices and theory to their management behaviors and strategies using prescribed sets of professional standards which are often referred to as "competencies." The program is a comprehensive course of study by which public managers can acquire and apply best practices and theory to their management behaviors and strategies using prescribed sets of seven professional competencies.

The curriculum uses theory as the foundation and applies it to practical problems facing the participant, their agency/department and the citizens (Balanoff, 2017). Since 1979, the National Certified Public Manager Consortium – an independent nonprofit organization – has been assigned the task of developing and preserving national standards, or competencies, for CPM designation, as well as providing a formal mechanism for accreditation (National Certified Public Manager Consortium, n.d.).

CPM is open to managers in federal, state and local government agencies. Some states also open enrollment to nonprofit organizations. The curriculum covers:

- Personal and Organizational Integrity: Increasing awareness, building skills and modeling behaviors related to identifying potential ethical problems and conflicts of interest; appropriate workplace behavior; and legal and policy compliance.
- Managing Work: Meeting organizational goals through effective planning, prioritizing, organizing and aligning human, financial, material and information resources. Empowering others by delegating clear job expectations; providing meaningful feedback and coaching; creating a motivational environment and measuring performance. Monitoring workloads and documenting performance. Dealing effectively with performance problems.
- Leading People: Inspiring others to positive action through a clear vision; promotes a diverse workforce. Encouraging and facilitating cooperation, pride, trust and group identity; fostering commitment and team spirit. Articulating a vision, ideas and facts in a clear and organized way; effectively managing emotions and impulses.
- Developing Self: Demonstrating commitment to continuous learning, self-awareness and individual performance planning through feedback, study and analysis.
- Systemic Integration: Approaching planning, decision making and implementation from an enterprise perspective; understanding internal and external relationships that impact the organization.
- Public Service Focus: Delivering superior services to the public and internal and external recipients; including customer/client identification, expectations, needs and developing and implementing paradigms, processes and procedures that exude positive spirit and climate; demonstrating agency and personal commitment to quality service.
- Change Leadership: Acting as a change agent; initiating and supporting change within the organization by implementing strategies to help others adapt to changes in the work environment, including personal reactions to change; emphasizing and fostering creativity and innovation; being proactive.

An even broader set of public management competencies across public administration programs, certificates and courses, including CPM, includes seven types of Executive Leadership Competencies (Box 5.4) (Illiash, 2013).

BOX 5.4   EXECUTIVE LEADERSHIP COMPETENCIES

Cluster 1: Personal Fundamentals

This cluster of competencies is comprised of those individual skills, traits and abilities that serve as a foundation – indeed as a necessary prerequisite – for success in demonstrating all other public leadership competencies covered in the model:

Interpersonal Skills
- Listening
- Trust Building
- Tact/Diplomacy
- Ability to Facilitate Groups
- "Selling" Ideas

Communication
- Oral Communication
  - Public Presentations
  - Technical Data Presentations
  - Fluency in Foreign Language(s)
  - Meeting Management
- Written Communication
  - Technical Report Writing
  - Grant Writing
  - Proposal Writing
  - Memo Writing under Deadline
  - In-depth Research Reports

Integrity/Honesty
- Professionalism
- Ethics
- Morality

Continual Learning

Attributes
- Analytic Skills
- Conceptual Thinking
- Capability for Systems Thinking

- Information Seeking
- Range of Interests
- Attention to Detail

Perception of Self
- Self-awareness
- Self-management
- Self-esteem

Need for Achievement

Cluster 2: Leading Change

This group of competencies "involves the ability to bring about strategic change, both within and outside the organization, to meet organizational goals"; it focuses on the "ability to establish an organizational vision and to implement it in a continuously changing environment" (United States Office of Personnel Management, 2010; ECQ Leading Change):

Creativity & Innovation
- Understanding Creative Processes
- Innovation: Framing the Issue
- Innovation and Organizational Environment

External Awareness
- Political Awareness
- Public Policymaking
- Environment of Public Administrative Agencies
- Scanning the Environment

Flexibility
- Components of Flexibility
- Guidelines to Flexibility
- Situational Leadership

Resilience
- Defining Resilience
- Sub-elements of Resilience
- Guidelines to Achieving and/or Sustaining Resilience

Vision, Mission & Strategic Thinking
- Defining Vision: the What, When, Why and Who

- Articulating the Mission
- Strategic Thinking

Managing Organizational Change
- Organizational Change: Definitions & Response
- Change Management Process
- Challenges and Models of Organizational Change Interventions in the Public Sector

Cluster 3: Leading People

This cluster describes a group of the so-called "people-oriented" competencies such as team building, managing conflict, leveraging diversity, motivating and developing others. These "soft" interventions are critical to successful leadership and are sometimes considered synonymous with it. They can also be called culture-creating competencies. With workforces becoming more multicultural and multi-generational, leaders will have to focus more of their attention on organizational culture creation to "accommodate at least some of the essential values and expectations of these disparate employee cultures along with their own"; the essence of this cluster of competencies is for a leader "to find ways to merge the age-old universal human drive to maximize personal need satisfaction with the needs of the organization" (Fairholm, 2011, p. 24).

Leadership

Team Building
- Teamwork and Cooperation
- Team Leadership

Leveraging Diversity
- Cross-cultural Leadership
- Diversity with Inclusion

Conflict Management
- Dispute Resolution
- Mediation

Developing Others
- Facts/Strategies/Development
- Evaluation
- Implementation

Work Motivation
*   Public Service Motivation
*   Empowering Others
*   Inspiring Others
*   Primacy of Work
*   History, Philosophy, Values & Beliefs

Cluster 4: Results Driven

This group of competencies involves the ability to meet organizational goals of high performance – and customer satisfaction in the delivery of those services. Performance programs include improvements in capacity, objective measures of outputs and outcomes, the identification and application of innovations, problem-solving partnerships with employees, reporting to policymakers and citizens, and overall strategic planning. Contributing competencies include:

Accountability
*   Understanding Accountability
*   Dimensions of Accountability
*   Accountability and the NPM

Performance Management/Performance Measurement
*   What Is Performance Management
*   Performance Measurement
*   Methodological Aspects of Developing Performance Measurement Systems

Customer Service
*   Government Performance as Customer Service
*   Commitment to Quality & Continuous Improvement
*   Applicability of Quality Management

Decisiveness
*   Decisiveness Defined
*   Guidelines for Diagnosing a Decision Situation
*   Guidelines to Achieving Decisiveness

Entrepreneurship
*   Entrepreneurship: Defined, Interpreted & Compared
*   Components of Entrepreneurship
*   Entrepreneurial Environment

Cluster 5: Process Driven

This cluster focuses on a group of competencies comprising the "task" domain of leadership, competencies considered fundamental in managing day-to-day operations of public agencies. By providing public sector leaders with the ability to apply technical knowledge and problem analysis, this cluster enables them to make decisions that produce high-quality results.

Problem Solving
- Application of Analytical & Administrative Tools to Solutions of Public Problems

Decision Making
- Cost-benefit Analysis
- Decision Analysis

Technical Credibility
- Discipline Leadership/Excellence
- Discipline Credibility
- Policies and Regulations
- Formal Organizational Structure
- Quantitative & Qualitative Design Methodology
- Systems and Procedures Analysis
- Organizational Culture
- Administrative Law
- Process Management and Organizational Design
- Organizational Development
- Labor Management Relations
- Job Analysis
- Stakeholder Analysis

Program/Project Management
- Operations Planning
- Manages Workflow
- Organizing, Planning and Implementing
- Management Systems and Processes

Cluster 6: Resource Acumen

This group of competencies is required to carry out structural responsibilities related to the organization – budgeting and financial management, human resources management, as well as information technology. As underscored by Van Wart, this group of competencies embodies the ability of the public sector leader "to build and maintain the management infrastructure and coordinate the various systems of the organization." He also indicated that, perceived as purely management functions, these competencies are typically missing from discussions of leadership while at the same time playing a critical role in highly regulated public bureaucracies (Van Wart, 2005):

Budgeting & Financial Management
- Financial Management
- Resource Allocation
- Budget Formulation and Analysis
- Asset Management
- Donations Management

Human Capital Management
- Staffing and Recruiting
- Succession Planning
- Personnel Systems Management
- Personnel Assessment
- Strategic Human Resource Practices
- Supervision
- Delegation
- Managing Personnel Change
- Consulting
- Volunteers

Technology Management
- IT Management
- Knowledge Capture & Sharing
- Management Information Systems

Cluster 7: Building Coalitions

This cluster includes a group of competencies that address internal and external cooperation and coalition building necessary to achieve common goals. Rooted in the notions of shared values and responsibility, these are the competencies that relate to what Luke (1998) calls inter-sectoral management or what today becomes known as collaborative leadership:

Adeptness in Coalition Building
- Establishes Collaborative Relationships & Projects

- Able to Network Effectively
- International Policy
- Inspiring Trust

Political Savvy
- Able to Analyze Political Support and Opposition
- Understands Community Building
- Law, Policy & Governance
- Organizational Advocacy
- Organizational Culture
- Organizational Awareness
- Perception of Threshold Social Cues
- Political Values and Processes
- Environmental Factors & Resource Availabilities

Influencing/Negotiating
- Able Negotiator
- Use of Socialized Power
- Facilitating & Gaining Cooperation and Partnerships
- Strategic Influencing
- Mobilizing Support, Creating Energizing Environments & Being a Conductor

This knowledge base of competencies is well developed and accessible. But it would be naive to expect their "delivery" via widespread enrollment in credit-bearing degree programs or in certificates. Public administrators and managers are typically busy people leading critical programs and projects who have neither the time nor the inclination to pursue a CPM program, which normally takes two years. Public administration could, however, pursue additional creative initiatives in order to avail all leaders of the full range of competencies:

- Require, by law, that all career public managers – and those aspiring to such positions – complete an online "Certificate of Public Management" within X months of their appointments.
- Distill the knowledge base for each of the seven competencies into an online program of one-hour segments totaling no more than 7–8 hours, including short video cases, that can introduce careerists and top-level political appointees (who are likely to serve government for just a few years), to the core Executive Leadership Competencies.

- Complement that program with a "review set" of bullet point suggestions and questions that they can call up on their computers, tablets or phones. This will enable them to access a checklist quickly – even in the midst of a meeting.
- Push no cost or low cost follow-up resources to them through newsletters, guides, blogs, videos, case studies, selections from the humanities, etc.
- Confront the problem that research findings as to the practice of public administration and management are virtually opaque to practitioners. For instance, brief synopses of journal articles could be compiled and published as options for improving organizational performance.

TAKEAWAYS

- The business model signals expectations that government should utilize efficient methods.
- Good Government organizations continue to contribute to government's capacities, now defined beyond efficiency in terms of ethics, effectiveness and impacts.
- The field of public administration has built a strong professionalized public service.
- The public sector has stepped in to continue services that the private sector could no longer profitably produce.
- Government expenditures are investments in services that enhance the quality of life for all citizens and the profitability of the private sector for all businesses.
- The efficacy of the privatization model is a myth, diverting resources and transgressing on public values.
- Public administration is distinctly different and more complex than the management of the private sector.
- A government vs. government public competition model can deliver the benefits of competition within the scope of public sector values.
- All public administrators and managers should be equipped with knowledge of the full range of competencies necessary to manage the public sector.

SELECTIONS FOR FURTHER READING AND RESEARCH

Bowman, J.S., West, J.P. and Beck, M.A. (2010) *Achieving Competencies in Public Service*. Armonk, NY: M.E. Sharpe.
Addresses the universal requisites for three sets of core competencies that all public sector leaders must acquire.

Cohen, D. and Mikaelian, A. (2021) *The Privatization of Everything: How the Plunder of Public Goods Transformed America and How We Can Fight Back.* New York and London: The New Press. (Also available as a C-SPAN Video, February 2022.) Powerful critique of the erosion of public values as the unavoidable byproducts created by privatization of public services.

Cordelli, Chiara (2022) *The Privatized State: Why Government Outsourcing of Public Powers Is Making Us Less Free.* Princeton, NJ: Princeton University Press. Compelling argument that privatization undermines our political institutions, and suggests remedies.

Grossman, S.A. and Holzer, M. (2015) *Partnership Governance in Public Management: A Public Solutions Handbook.* New York and London: Routledge. Public-private partnerships, rather than privatization, is an intersectoral win-win innovation that can complement the strengths, and compensate for the weaknesses, of each partnering organization, all in the public interest.

Holzer, M. and Fry, J.C. (2011) *Shared Services and Municipal Consolidation – a Critical Analysis.* Newark, NJ: National Center for Public Performance. Consolidation, centralization and regionalization are potentially productive alternatives to traditional government silos.

Mazzucato, M. (2013) *The Entrepreneurial State: Debunking Public vs. Private Sector Myths.* New York and London: Anthem Press. Convincingly argues that the public sector is the leading edge of innovation, making high-risk investments from which the private sector often profits.

Norman-Major, K.A. and Gooden, S.T. (2012) *Cultural Competency for Public Administrators.* New York and London: Routledge. Present "cultural competency" as a contemporary and necessary sensitivity that must be factored into budget priorities and program implementation.

Quinn, R.E., St. Clair, L.S., Faerman, S.R., Thompson, M. and McGrath, M.R. (2020) *Becoming a Master Manager: A Competing Values Approach.* Seventh edition, Hoboken, NJ: Wiley. Master of the "competing values framework" empowers public, nonprofit and private sector managers to deliver promised results.

REFERENCES

Allison, G.T. (1980) *Public and Private Management: Are They Fundamentally Alike in All Unimportant Respects?* Cambridge, MA: John F. Kennedy School of Government, Harvard University.

Balanoff, H.R. (2017, August 30) The National Certified Public Manager® (CPM) Program: A model for public and nonprofit leaders and managers around the world. Paper presented at the European Group for Public Administration (EGPA)

Conference, Milan, Italy. http://gato-docs.its.txstate.edu/jcr:fcda9c10-0702-4be7-b446-8ba7abb133f4/EGPA%20Paper%20Rev%20Aug%2012%202017.pdf

Cherry, R.L. and Dave, D.S. (1997) An application of outcomes assessments to measure effectiveness of graduate courses in a United States business school. *International Journal of Management*, 14(4), 646–53.

Cohen, D. and Mikaelian, A. (2021) *The Privatization of Everything: How the Plunder of Public Goods Transformed America and How We Can Fight Back*. New York and London: The New Press.

Cordelli, C. (2020, November 24) Why privatization is wrong. *The Boston Review*. https://bostonreview.net/articles/chiara-cordelli-harms-privatization/

Coughlin, T.A., Long, S.K., Clemans-Cope, L. and Resnick, D. (2013, May) *What Difference Does Medicaid Make? Assessing Cost Effectiveness, Access, and Financial Protection under Medicaid for Low-income Adults*. Washington, DC: Kaiser.

Dahlberg, J.S. (1966) *The New York Bureau of Municipal Research, Pioneer in Government Administration*. New York: New York University Press.

Dorfman, A. and Harel, A. (2015, November 25) Against privatisation as such. Oxford Journal of Legal Studies, 36(2), 400–27.

Fairholm, G.W. (2011) *Real Leadership: How Spiritual Values Give Leadership Meaning*. Santa Barbara, CA: Praeger.

Federal Commission on Military, National and Public Service (2020). https://www.federalregister.gov/agencies/national-commission-on-military-national-and-public-service and https://hasbrouck.org/draft/FOIA/STAFF-MEMORANDUM-UNIVERSAL-SERVICE.pdf

Fehrer, D.G. (2020, October 21) Federal Salary Council meeting minutes Meeting Number 20-01. U.S. Office of Personnel Management. https://www.opm.gov/policy-data-oversight/pay-leave/pay-systems/general-schedule/minutes/20-01-fsc-minutes.pdf

Goodnow, F.J. (1900) *Politics and Administration: A Study in Government*. New York: Macmillan.

Harvey, J.T. (2012, October 2) Why government should not be run like a business. *Forbes*. https://www.forbes.com/sites/johntharvey/2012/10/05/government-vs-business/

Holzer, M. (with Roberts, B. and Wexler, J) (2018) *A Call to Serve: Quotes on Public Service*. Washington, DC: American Society for Public Administration.

Holzer, M. and Fry, J.C. (2011) *Shared Services and Municipal Consolidation – a Critical Analysis*. Newark, NJ: National Center for Public Performance.

Holzer, M. and Lin, W. (2007, Spring–Summer) A longitudinal perspective on MPA education in the United States. *Journal of Public Affairs Education*, 13(2), 345–64.

Illiash, I. (2013) Constructing an integrated model of public-sector leadership competencies: An exploration (Doctoral dissertation). Newark, NJ: Rutgers University Graduate School.

Kerr, E., and Wood, S. (2022, June 8) The cost of public vs. private colleges. *U.S. News & World Report*. Retrieved September 13, 2022, from https://www.usnews.com/education/best-colleges/paying-for-college/articles/2019-06-25/the-cost-of-private-vs-public-colleges

Lazenby, S. (2010, September) The adequacy of MPA course content in preparing local government managers. *Journal of Public Affairs Education*, 16(3), 337–60.

Luke, J.S. (1998) *Catalytic Leadership: Strategies for an Interconnected World*. San Francisco, CA: Jossey-Bass Publishers.

Mohler, J. (2019, January 17). After 3 decades, privatization has been proven a failure. Let's bury it for good. *In These Times*. https://inthesetimes.com/article/privatization -alexandria-ocasio-cortez-rich-charter-schools-healthcare

National Certified Public Manager Consortium (n.d.) What is a Certified Public Manager. Retrieved September 12, 2022, from https://cpmconsortium.org/What-is -a-Certified-Public-Manager

Public Citizen (n.d.) Top 10 reasons to oppose water privatization. Retrieved September 12, 2022, from https://www.citizen.org/wp-content/uploads/top10-reasonstooppo sewaterprivatization.pdf

Rainey, H.G., Backoff, R.W. and Levine, C.H. (1976) Comparing public and private organizations. *Public Administration Review*, 36(2), 233–44.

Reagan, R. (1982, March 3) Remarks at the Los Angeles County, California, Board of Supervisors' Town Meeting. *The American Presidency Project*. https://www .presidency.ucsb.edu/documents/remarks-the-los-angeles-county-california-board -supervisors-town-meeting

Reagan, R. (1983, August 2) Remarks at a White House briefing for administration offi-cials on federal management reform. *The American Presidency Project*. https://www .presidency.ucsb.edu/documents/remarks-white-house-briefing-for-administration -officials-federal-management-reform

Riccucci, N.M. (2010) *Public Administration: Traditions of Inquiry and Philosophies of Knowledge*. Washington, DC: Georgetown University Press.

Savas, E.S. (1992) It's time to privatize. *Fordham Urban Law Journal*, 19(3), 781–94. https://ir.lawnet.fordham.edu/cgi/viewcontent.cgi?referer=&httpsredir=1&article= 1563&context=ulj

Sayre, W. (1958) Premises of public administration: Past and emerging. *Public Administration Review*, 18(2), 102–5.

Schachter, H. (2002) Philadelphia's progressive-era Bureau of Municipal Research. *Administrative Theory & Praxis*, 24(3).

Schachter, H. (2005) Public productivity in the Classical Age. In M. Holzer and S.-H. Lee (eds), *Public Productivity Handbook*. New York: Marcel Dekker.

United States Office of Personnel Management (2010, June) Guide to senior executive service qualifications. https://www.opm.gov/policy-data-oversight/senior-executive -service/reference-materials/guidetosesquals_2010.pdf

Van Slyke, D.M. (2003, May–June) The mythology of privatization in contracting for social services. *Public Administration Review*, 63(3).

Van Wart, M. (2005) *Dynamics of Leadership in Public Service: Theory and Practice*. Armonk, NY: M.E. Sharpe.

von Mises, L. (2017) Why businessmen fail at government. Excerpt from *Bureaucracy, 1944. Fee Stories*. May 18, 2017.

Wilson, W. (1887, June) The study of administration. *Political Science Quarterly*, 2(2), 197–222.

6. A comeback for the administrative state: an agenda going forward

Going forward, the field of public administration must address key concerns that threaten the future of government, indeed the future of governance. Addressing those concerns is important to society's compact with its citizens, but only if the administrative state asserts its legitimacy as part of an increasingly complex set of tools for protecting and improving the quality of life for over 300 million people in the US. In *The Administrative State*, Waldo presented a powerful argument for the necessary role that agencies assume as executive branch implementers of public policy, as the President's agents. Our contemporary society requires an administrative framework that can build out broad policies by rules and regulations, by exercising discretion, and all the while respecting democratic values (Waldo, 1948 [2006]). To assert that legitimacy, the accomplishments of the public sector must be salient to the public and their media and political surrogates. Public administration, seemingly challenged at all levels of government, must differentiate itself from the associated and demeaning labels of "bureaucracy," "deep state" and "shadow government" by confronting ten core concerns.

First, public trust is the foundational issue. Public organizations must reverse the trend of declining trust, must reach the public with clear and comprehensive evidence that establishes their primacy as society's best investments. Public organizations prevent disease, keep the peace, protect the food supply, educate future generations, and respond to emergencies small and large. They accomplish scores of other missions. The recent pandemic- and economic-related crises have reaffirmed the importance of government in everyday terms. Trust is the "glue" for governing societies, conferring upon government its basic source of power and its tax-provided budgetary resources. Yet despite a set of sterling accomplishments, declining budgets are a function of a trust deficiency. A breakdown in the civic contract undermines the ability of governments to continue to perform at high levels, to deliver services as promised in their founding documents, their legislation, their agency mission statements and the oaths of office sworn to by their public servants.

Distrust of government is often a debate of extremes, of virtually no action to remediate a problems versus an activist approach: for example, leaving health insurance or housing completely to the market, or providing hybrid public-private markets administered by the bureaucracy. Often a workable solution is incremental, to solve the most critical problems that need to be solved first, allowing everyone to save face and plan for the future. This means embracing a time-honored, often mocked, but just as often highly effective mechanism: the bipartisan commission. A bipartisan set of experts – including civil servants as well as legislators who characteristically play important roles in finding solutions to politicized debates – could objectively and independently assess the full range of strategies that have been identified for ameliorating a particular problem. That assessment would inform decisions within the next financial year. These studies would be multidimensional and international, with a goal of prioritizing possible investments and expenditures. Our society thrives on science, facts and expertise. Many experts within the executive branch stand ready to answer those questions dispassionately and apolitically.

Second, the role of government has been trending toward invisibility, as is often the case when the increased use of nongovernmental contractors (both the private sector and NGOs) to deliver public services gives rise to doubts as to the very need for a public bureaucracy. While much of the New Public Management movement was designed to "restore" trust in government through better productivity and performance, the concomitant blurring of the distinction between the public and private sectors may paradoxically have created more distrust. Citizens have become confused as to who represents their interests, where to register requests and complaints, and why they are paying fees on top of taxes.

Third, we need to consider how public organizations might reestablish their legitimacy – the acceptance or acquiescence of the government and its public servants by the polity in terms of both necessary and desired services. Agencies must clearly communicate "how" public services are delivered, the performance of public sector agencies in delivering those services, the level and type of participation by citizens, and the flow of information from government to its citizens. Transparency and accountability must be practiced throughout government. The same ethical principles that apply to public officials must apply to their nongovernmental partners who deliver government-funded services and are typically misidentified by the public as government bureaucrats. The more open government is perceived to be, the greater the likelihood that trust will rebound.

Fourth, government's many simultaneous missions, all within collective resource constraints known as "budgets," require delicate balancing acts. This gives rise to tensions: short-term versus long-term commitments; balancing the welfare state with conservative fiscal responsibility; and realistic expectations for carefully constructed programs versus instant gratification as promised by pandering politicians. Public sector organizations face simultaneous commitments: keeping the economic house in order despite global crises and unavoidable cycles; maintaining legitimacy and satisfying citizens despite often unrealistic expectations; and coping with crises, such as a pandemic, in a world where citizens question science and fact-based public health mandates. The field of public administration, charged with "solving" such difficult crises, must make the case to other actors, such as school systems and universities, and in partnership with other fields such as political science and public health, that all students – indeed all citizens – need to be educated in causal reasoning, benefit-cost relationships, how to make sense of graphic displays of data, the red flags of false "research," and an understanding of civics.

Fifth, disciplinary silos must be breached. Governance has, of course, been studied not only by public administration scholars, but also by researchers from other disciplines such as economics, business management, political science and sociology. Public administration as a field, however, is inadequately incorporating the contributions of other disciplines into debates and analyses about governance. The field has paid virtually no attention to lessons from literature and the arts, critiques that are evident in novels, in movies and on small screens. Bringing those ethical and client-generated insights into the dialogue is essential to developing broader and deeper lessons for the field. We should welcome boundary-spanning dialogues in the context of addressing messy problems, such as public health threats; climate change; immigration driven by cataclysmic events, natural and manmade; pollution of the seas; intellectual property appropriation; human trafficking; market manipulations and many other problems that continually bedevil society. It is government's mission to confront those problems, and government needs broader, multidisciplinary perspectives in order to do so.

Sixth is the extent to which rational executive behavior is a naive assumption. Market-like mechanisms assume rationality in the behaviors of government's stakeholders. Rational decision-making expectations must always be tempered, however, by the "inexplicable and irrational" behaviors exhibited in decision making, from street-level bureaucrats to their clients and stakeholders. Public leadership styles may, unfortunately, be more a function of informal assumptions than of informed research and may be grounded in ungrounded "common sense" rather than fact-based observations. "Management by whim at the White House" (Box 6.1) is a case in point. Many other instances of whimsical decisions are regularly reported.

BOX 6.1   MANAGEMENT BY WHIM AT THE WHITE HOUSE

John F. Kennedy's careful decision making brought the Cuban Missile Crisis to a safe, enduring conclusion. Seeking balanced, informed advice, he convened the "ExCom" of cabinet-level advisors to stop a seemingly inevitable rush to nuclear war. The lesson, often ignored, is that effective leadership comes not from the belly but from the brain. The reality is that presidents who have headed off conflicts or managed complex situations have done so with great respect for professional advice and an openness to alternative points of view.

Abraham Lincoln valued his Cabinet's "team of rivals" in bringing a complex and catastrophic war to a conclusion. Woodrow Wilson's "Fourteen Points" of War Aims and Peace Terms in 1918 was a blueprint for world peace produced by "The Inquiry" team of well over a hundred political and social scientists. Franklin Roosevelt's "brain trust" of academic advisors, respected for their wide-ranging expertise, helped him achieve dramatic initiatives in recovering from the Great Depression. Barack Obama brought together a broad coalition of senior executives and foreign allies in developing the Iran Nuclear agreement.

But contrary to those collective efforts, the undying myth that a President must be a decisive, iconoclastic actor is again being acted out tragically in Washington. Like Shakespeare's King Lear, insecure residents of the White House, the Kremlin or palaces worldwide have taken it upon themselves to lead their countries into dangerous situations by practicing "management by whim."

Donald Trump was supposedly emulating his predecessors, "deciders" Ronald Reagan and George W. Bush. But Reagan acted hastily, without adequate military intelligence data, to invade Grenada. Bush acted on false intelligence about weapons of mass destruction (WMDs) to invade Iraq. Both invasions – like the US morass in Vietnam – would not have gone forward if the ExCom model or similar groups of seasoned advisors, such as the National Security Council, had been able to place confirmed intelligence on the table in the Situation Room, and if those reviews had been considered with open minds.

Trump was unparalleled in having brought a distinct impatience and distrust of professionals to the Oval Office. His uninformed, unexamined and unrealistic decisions produced a litany of slowly developing disasters: the acceleration, rather than deceleration, of climate change; the spread, rather than early suppression, of COVID-19 to pandemic proporations; abuse, rather than care, for migrant children in government custody at the southern

border; more missiles and nuclear bombs in North Korea; etc. This was neither a game nor a movie. This was an existential situation in which the Chief
Executive imagined he was shrewder than anyone else, that his gut-level
decisions were more powerful than those of his predecessors or rivals. In
truth, he was not inquisitive enough to seek professional advice or to open
his decisions to proficient scrutiny.

Seventh is whether we are adequately improving performance in government
in order to "deliver as promised." Instead of reforms just modeled on private
sector practices – the business model or privatization – public administration
research and practice should focus on rational analyses which entail information collection and are used to support fact-based decision making. Instead of
publishing data only in off-putting spreadsheets and tables, performance measures should be presented as graphics that are readily understandable. Instead
of casually imagining solutions to organizational problems, governments and
their elected leaders should be searching the web for best practices, and then
adapting those innovations to the local context. Overall, government should
give much more weight to performance data that speak to goal achievement.

Eighth, emerging technologies actually have a very positive effect on governance by giving rise to new forms of public deliberation and collaboration –
blogs, social media, podcasts, apps, smart phones. But just as important are the
unintended and negative consequences of those technologies. New forms of
governance could extend to the use of web-based tools for citizen and agency
deliberation, and co-development of public policy mandates and regulations
via extensive online conversations with stakeholders. New communication
technologies and social media enable more robust public engagement over
public policy and program management issues, as well as new means of
internal organizational teamwork. Web technologies allow for coordination,
collaboration and process integration, as well as citizen services and opportunities for public deliberation. The internet and its technological offerings are
rapidly evolving, and with every new tool there are promises, limitations and
unintended consequences.

Those consequences extend to the very nature of public administration
research. Is qualitative research fading as the ease of access to databases and
related analytical methods grows exponentially? Are we losing thoughtful,
observational insights to formulaic, data-driven articles that produce relatively
narrow conclusions but are the "coin of the realm" for peer-reviewed research?
We need both qualitative and quantitative published research, but the latter is
often inaccessible or unpalatable to practitioners. Perhaps we need to emulate
the popular publications and networks in the fields of business and health
administration that are clearly written and pitched toward practitioners.

The field is also impacted unintentionally by virtual communications. Webinars are a plus, with the potential to multiply academic-practitioner and practitioner-practitioner dialogues as well as dissemination of knowledge. But there may be downsides to related technologies. Will virtual conferences change the nature of interactions toward less substance and more superficiality? Will a movement toward many more online classes downgrade MPA education? The full and systemic implications of technology across the field need to be subjected to systematic and objective research.

Ninth, and often overlooked, is the need for professional collaboration and extensive networking in the course of complex and shifting human interactions. In a "work at home" era, we have an inadequate understanding of collaboration, hybrid governance and networking. What are the main concerns that theory and research must address in an increasingly digital work environment: Erosion of networking and promotional opportunities for those working at home? Inadequate collaboration and networking in a purely digital environment? Loss of meaningful input and feedback from public servants and clients? Skewed participation in stakeholder networks characterized by temporary "pop up" links and "instant" polls?

Tenth, can we staff the public service in order to address the nine preceding questions? There is anecdotal evidence that public service as a career is on the upswing, that more undergraduates are considering careers in the public sector, and more seasoned professionals are opting out of the private sector, transitioning to public sector and not-for-profit careers. Although public service is an exceptionally rewarding career path, simple assumptions and stereotypes may limit the career possibilities of anyone entering government or the many not-for-profits that deliver government services. The field needs to build its visibility as a career destination; too many undergraduates have never heard of public administration, or MPA. They default in their career choices to business administration, the MBA. But in South Korea the MPA is much more prevalent. If public administration is to thrive, then academics and practitioners need to highlight career choices, best practices and the best public servants who make possible high-performing government.

Technology can assist in advocating for careers in public service, and an emerging example is the Virtual Museum of Public Service (Box 6.2). This project would highlight many of the arguments presented in this book, thereby contributing not only to rethinking, but to rebuilding, the public sector.

BOX 6.2   VIRTUAL MUSEUM OF PUBLIC SERVICE: HONORING DEDICATION TO THE PUBLIC GOOD

The Proposed Project

The Virtual Museum of Public Service (VMPS) will offer engaging, in-depth, multimedia exhibits that highlight the positive roles public servants, institutions and their partners have played in delivering on government's promises to the public. These public servants and institutions have immeasurably improved the quality of life for all stakeholders across the realms of health, education, the arts, criminal justice, defense, security, and dozens of other services that build social capital.

We define public servants broadly as employees or volunteers in government (civilian and military), nonprofits, public-private partnerships, foundations, the media and voluntary organizations.

Each exhibit in the museum's collection will be accompanied by in-depth explanatory articles, extensive lists of bibliographic and further reading materials, and multimedia links to related online resources. Additionally, the museum will utilize its connections with public service-oriented academics and practitioners worldwide to produce high school and college-level lesson plans related to museum holdings. In this way, the museum will act as a novel global resource for students, educators, researchers, leaders and policymakers interested in the experiences, sacrifices and successes of public servants.

The Rationale

In an environment where the work and sacrifices of public servants are not always celebrated, the VMPS sets out to remind and to inform the general public about the scope, range and ethos of public service. The VMPS believes that many museum visitors will be surprised to learn about how much their fellow citizens in the public service accomplish with relatively sparse funding and resources.

Over 30 million Americans currently work in the public service – in the military and in federal, state and local government. Moreover, millions of nonprofit partners and private sector contractors, as well as media reporters and foundation staff, help these public servants carry out the missions of government; most have not been recognized as public servants in their own right. The museum will serve as a vehicle through which all of these individuals can celebrate the legacies of public servants who risked their lives and careers to ensure the equitable delivery of supportive services before them. The museum will stress the importance of public servants' historical and current contributions, and their quiet pride in serving their fellow citizens.

Objectives

The public sector is broadly reflected in the arts and in contemporary media, yet its endeavors are often oversimplified and tainted in the headlines or the movies as "bureaucratic" or "inefficient." These stereotypes have contributed to a steady decline in respect for the work of, and funding for, public servants over the last 50 years or more. The failure to celebrate the work of public servants has had the debilitating effect of deterring promising students from careers in the public sector.

As a tool for teaching and learning, the Virtual Museum of Public Service (VMPS.US) will work to reverse these trends. The museum seeks to speak to and inspire:

- public and nonprofit employees,
- high school students fulfilling community service requirements, and college students who are committed to pursuing post-graduate careers in public service,
- young people interested in becoming more engaged citizens,
- members of the media, who are often de facto public servants,
- foundation staff who help carry out the work of governments and nonprofits.

Gallery A: The Foundations of Public Service

The Architecture and Public Works exhibit highlights both memorials and public venues that serve important historical, symbolic and cultural functions, as well as a broad array of improvement projects that ensure that individuals have safe and reliable infrastructure to use in the public sphere. Serving the Public in Elected Office highlights influential political leaders at the federal, state and local levels of government who have been driven by an intrinsic desire to contribute to the common good.

Gallery B: Public Service, Dangerous Service

Despite its perceived generous benefits and job security, a public service career can often be challenging and even dangerous. The exhibits in this wing – Security, Fire and Emergency Management, Military Service, Public

Safety and Law Enforcement, Criminal Justice and Investigative Services
– celebrate those public servants willing to place themselves in harm's way
in order to facilitate the safe and efficient functioning of the public sphere.
Some public service occupations that might be stereotyped as "safe" will
also have dedicated spaces in this gallery, occupations such as: teaching, li-
brarianship, nursing, public health providers and postal service employees.

Gallery C: Education, Libraries & the Helping Professions

Governmental and nonprofit educational organizations are foundational institutions that promote public values day in and day out. Education,
Libraries and the Helping Professions celebrates these institutions as accessible gateways to knowledge and culture, presenting biographical information on those who have had influential careers as librarians, or philanthropists who contributed to enhancing the role of libraries in the lives of their
community members. Social Work and the Helping Professions highlights
professionals who have, throughout history, nurtured the growth of individuals' psychological, intellectual, emotional or spiritual wellbeing, whether
through medicine, nursing, therapy, counseling, social work, education.

Gallery D: Science and Service to the Public

Public institutions are at the center of upholding and improving human
health and sustaining our environment, though their impact is often over-
shadowed by polarizing policy debates. The Science and Service to the
Public exhibit highlights the administrators, biologists, conservationists,
activists, ecologists and other natural scientists who survey changes in our
natural world and advocate for the protection of our environment. Public
Health and Healthcare showcases the history of organizations and public
health professionals that strive every day to deliver services to protect the
health of our families and communities, whether working in hospitals, nursing homes, schools or mental health facilities.

Gallery E: Diversity in Public Service

Diversity is essential to the health of the public sector. The galleries in this
wing explore the vital contributions of people of color, women, immigrants,
LGBTQ+ individuals, and others from underrepresented groups. These galleries aim to illuminate the importance of diverse voices. Their importance
in shaping the systems and structures that surround us have often gone unrecognized. The galleries in this wing also explore leadership, motivation
and innovation, influential factors that have shaped the public service.

Gallery F: Public Management – Ideals into Actions

If not for the diligent work of public administrators, legislated policy ideals would be just ideas. By implementing those ideas via action, public managers at all levels of government and nonprofits are essential to the delivery of public services and, therefore, to public satisfaction. This gallery offers visual insights into numerous perspectives on public management. In Financing our Common Purposes, we examine taxation as a means of fulfilling the common good. International Public Service examines boundary-spanning organizations that aim to address issues affecting the worldwide wellbeing.

Special Exhibits

Journalism
In 1904, the trailblazing nineteenth-century Hungarian journalist, Joseph Pulitzer, used his will to establish an annual award that would celebrate excellence in US journalism. An early proponent of university-level training for journalists, Pulitzer saw journalism as a rigorous art form with a strong moral and ethical basis. Having himself been exceptionally bold in reporting on the corruption of American government and corporations in the late nineteenth century, he was eager to encourage other journalists to view their profession as a public service. Since 1917, the Pulitzer Public Service Awards have celebrated publications that demonstrate courage, honesty and transparency in keeping the public informed, no matter the weight of the information. Pulitzer understood that there could be no stable democracy without a free press and fearless storytellers.

Philanthropy: a core mission of public service
Philanthropy is an enduring mission, which comes in many forms o provide support for initiatives addressing the root causes of major global challenges: resource scarcities in small communities, and individual needs among the disabled and disadvantaged. Donors, whether large or small, also recognize the importance of giving more than money. Many are able to give non-financial assets, such as their influence to advance advocacy programs, contacts and networks to expand the reach of fundraising initiatives. The field of philanthropy also plays an important role in supporting experimental stages of innovative ideas, which when proven can be utilized and implemented by governments toward addressing public problems. Philanthropists are often at the helm of initiatives involving partnerships between public and private organizations as well as civil society.

Beyond exhibits, additional tools and resources offered by the museum will render the site a comprehensive resource for students, teachers, and researchers:

- An interactive timeline documenting critical dates in the history of public service will lend visitors an overarching sense of the historical trajectory and development of the conception of public service.
- A public service "News Room" will collate recent stories in the media which showcase both the positive work that public servants are engaged in globally and the hardships that they face.
- Data visualization tools and infographics used throughout the site will be used to help dispel some of the popular misconceptions surrounding the public service sector.
- The Voices of Public Leaders podcast will present interviews, talks and public comments by prominent leaders sharing perspectives, challenges and opportunities for the critical issues facing the public sector.
- The "Ask Me Why I Care" YouTube series will present video stories of public servants representing public safety, fire services, health and government.
- A comprehensive career/volunteer information page will allow visitors to explore ways in which they themselves can make a difference in the realm of public service.
- A Public Service YouTube Channel will archive engaging perspectives on public service, such as presidential speeches, excerpts from public service-oriented commencement addresses, and media scenes that present positive views of public service.
- Dedicated issues of the open-access journal *Public Voices* will highlight contemporary aspects of public service.

Source: Referenced May 23, 2023: https://www.publicservicemuseum.org/

Rethinking public administration boils down to thinking more openly, imaginatively, broadly and inclusively. For government to accomplish its missions, it must consciously develop a broader mindset, a larger toolbox, an abundance of partnerships and a plethora of compelling evidence. This book has attempted to identify the resources and logic models necessary for more effective government, for a public sector that delivers on the promises made in foundational documents. As a whole, this book presents strategic opportunities for the public sector to rebuild the public's trust. The ultimate test is whether public trust in government rebounds.

TAKEAWAYS

A series of win-win actions may markedly improve the outcomes that the public expects and that public servants signed on to deliver. We can reverse a declining spiral of trust if we:

- Emphasize and abide by the ethics of public service.
- Listen to our critics in the arts and humanities.
- Carefully consider the alerts and issues raised by bureaucratic resistors.
- Celebrate successes by documenting and communicating high personal and organizational performance.
- Emphasize sacrifices by public servants.
- Cast public service as a noble pursuit not only by those staffing government, but also those serving their fellow citizens in many other ways.
- Identify, highlight and "push" public service exemplars.
- Confront the assumptions of the "business model."
- Argue for universal mastery of the competencies necessary to run a government.

SELECTIONS FOR FURTHER READING AND RESEARCH

Rohr, J. (1986) *To Run a Constitution: The Legitimacy of the Administrative State.* Lawrence, KS: University Press of Kansas.
A very thoughtful perspective on the administrative state in the context of Constitutional theory.

REFERENCES

Virtual Museum of Public Service. Referenced May 23, 2023, https://www.publicservicemuseum.org/
Waldo, D. (2006) *The Administrative State: A Study of the Political Theory of American Public Administration.* New York and London: Routledge.

Index